£1

God's never offside

You have not only blessed me personally in buying this book (let's face it, if it were just my mum I could simply have phoned her!), but your money will make a difference in the life of someone else.

Half of all profits from the sales of **God's never offside** *are going to a project in Nigeria that I'm involved with. We're building a school and an orphanage in one of the country's poorest areas, Amawbia, in the eastern state of Anambra. Our aim is to alleviate some of the suffering and bring hope through Christian teaching and education.*

Thank you for helping, I pray you seek and find more of His love in each and every day – you deserve it.

God's never offside

Lorna Grady

Text copyright © 2005 Lorna Grady
lorna@issacharmedia.co.uk

Design and layout copyright © 2005 The Partnership Publishing Solutions Ltd
www.the-pps.co.uk

ISBN 1-9543683-1-2

Printed and bound by Bercker Graphischer Betrieb GmbH & Co, Germany

This book is dedicated to the wonderful memory of my dad,
Billy Farrell (1937–2004),
who taught me so much about kindness, contentment and bad
dancing. I loved you so much more than I ever knew.

Contents

Acknowledgements

Martin and Matthew: My two boys, the best, funniest, most amazing guys I know, I love you (sorry for the embarrassment!).

My family: Mum, Elaine and Shirley, we have been through it but emerged stronger, I love you always.

The Friends: Heather Farrell, Nicola Etherington, Shona Leishman and Carol Wallace. You're truly wonderful, beautiful friends and each a true blessing. I love you and always will. Thanks for *all* your support, prayers, finance, walks, talks, tears and flapjacks. You're the best.

David Cameron: To the most patient, encouraging, wise editor *ever*, but especially thank you for being the most gentle of shepherds. Thanks for your time and compassion, you know how far you've shared my journey; I'm eternally grateful and count you my friend before my minister!

Pastor Joe Nwokoye: For teaching me the answer to everything is in Scripture and for sharing your beautiful country with my heart. I love you, Pastor, sir!

Kirsty Bell and David Plews: For Wednesday nights long ago and valued friendships, thanks for being who you are.

Andrew Dougall: For your friendship, photos and web page, thanks for believing in me and helping dispel some of the fears, every blessing forever.

David Farrell: For your amazing kindness and having the most generous heart. From all the kids you've helped (including me), God bless you.

Kate Blackstock and my family in Oz: I love you guys, praise the Lord for the telephone!

Graeme Mathie: For listening during the darkest time, thanks for being shiny, love you forever.

Jack Geddes and Eleanor Jackson at The Partnership: Thanks for your endless patience, grace, coffee and comma removal. Thanks for making my words become a book; I really couldn't have done it without you. Jack – thanks for understanding my grief when I needed to talk.

Phil Starbuck, Dietmar Ness, Jaime Fernandez and Reuben Fernandez: Thank you for connecting me with the players I needed, may God bless the amazing work you do for Him.

Carol Patton at Rangers: For organising Bert so quickly for me.

Naheeda Phillips: For helping me choose Scripture and for teaching me what a generous spirit really is.

Robert Campbell: Thank you for rescuing me, and the book, from the nasty computer, bless you.

Graeme Lipsett: Thank you for smiling through the daftest computer queries; you're a true encourager.

Sunday night fellowship group: My brothers and sisters in Christ. Thank you for all the songs, prayers and the company into the Throne room. He is good!

Michael Antoniou: For Porsches, lunches, Harleys and decking, but above all, friendship and a heart for the underdog. Bless you.

Karen Graham: For being a wonderful messenger and an amazing support – His best for us both.

A special thank you to each of the twelve guys featured in the book that all gave me their time and thoughts, sometimes more than once. You're all stars and I'm truly blessed to have met each one of you. Thank you from the bottom of my heart and I pray God's blessing on you all as you continue to trust His unfailing love and compassion in your lives. You are real kingdom players!

Above all, I want to acknowledge the Holy Spirit who was with both the players and myself throughout the interviews and with me as I wrote. May all the glory and honour go to Him, forever.

Introduction

I love God, it's simple. I love football, that's simple too. What better two things to write about then than God and football? What better people to ask some questions of than footballers who love God?

This book writing seems pretty simple to me. I started writing this book because I wanted to share some facts and concerns about both; however, God quickly got involved and guided me in His chosen path (believe me, His version is much better than mine and I don't just mean the spelling!). This book aims to answer some of the questions that arise for all of us as we search for true meaning and love in our lives. It also illustrates how life as a professional footballer is a poor second to knowing God and all His plans for you.

Often people assume Christianity is a religion based on rules and restrictions, they think God is a killjoy intent on stopping any fun in this world. Christians according to some are geeks and weirdoes with no sense of humour or individuality, who, like clones, obey a God who can't be seen or heard, *wrong*! Christianity is about *relationship*, not rules. Yes, God has put boundaries and guidelines in place for us but He has given us free will that doesn't stop us ignoring Him.

Football is a game where players know the rules, respect them (or suffer the consequences!) and use their talents and skills to play well. The best and most exciting games to watch are not without rules or guidance, rather they are when players use all their skill, passion and talent within these guidelines to be the best they can be. God has given each of us talents, He has given us all a desire to find Him and follow Him, to come into a relationship where He is our Father and our friend.

Read this book with an open mind, the guys who are speaking aren't mutant clones with no opinions, far from it. They are united in one thing, their God is real and He is on their side, they can only ever win!

Let God speak to you through these words and thoughts, then let Him guide you into His team, let Him become real to you and receive His love. It might just change your life! Nothing major then!

He's always there for you, always supporting you, ready to pass and play, never shirking a tackle from the enemy yet never sidestepping the truth, quick to defend and shield you yet upfront and ready to set-up a strike for you, strong in the midfield and always in control, after all, *God's never offside*!

Lorna Grady
October 2005

Bert Konterman

DATE OF BIRTH: 14.11.71

POSITION: Central defender or midfielder

CLUB HISTORY: FC Zwolle, Cambuur, Willem II, Feijnoord, Rangers, Vitesse Arnhem

INTERNATIONAL HISTORY: Full caps for Holland

BEST EVER FOOTBALL MOMENT: In the semi-final of the 2002 CIS Cup against Celtic at Hampden, I scored the winning goal from approximately 30 yards during extra-time.

BEST EVER SPIRITUAL MOMENT: When I was around ten years old, with the help of my teacher at that time, I started realising that everything in life is controlled by *God* and *He* is our main goal in life.

FAVOURITE ALL-TIME FOOTBALL ELEVEN (*4/4/2 formation*):

		Dasaev		
Zanetti	Rijkaard		Maldini	Numan
Figo	Tigana		Zidane	Giggs
	Van Basten		Raul	

FAVOURITE PIECE OF SCRIPTURE: Romans is my favourite. I think it's the one book in the Bible that relates to today's society and world. Very understandable with examples from happenings in the modern world.

Bert Konterman
How do I know if I'm a Christian?

O kay, you always help old ladies across the road, put out the wheelie bin (if you're nagged enough), have never committed murder and to the best of your knowledge have never eaten a hungry kid's dinner, there, doesn't that make you a Christian? Sometimes it's hard to know exactly what a Christian is (apart from someone with an awful taste in tank tops!) and what they do, so how do you know?

One person who is in absolutely no doubt about who and what he is, is former Rangers defender, Bert Konterman. Having become a Christian at the age of ten, he was brought up in a Christian home, in a small village in Holland where the church was the centre of the community and he is clear in his mind about his faith in God, so how did he know he was a Christian?

> You come to the point where you believe in the Lord and you accept that God sent Jesus into this world to save us, to die for our sins. For me, you become a Christian when you realise God made us not just for this world, but there is life after. I know that my family, friends, football, etc are important to me, but I became a Christian when I realised that there was much more to life. The key for me was to realise that He has a plan for me, for my whole life and to believe in Him.

So, a Christian simply believes, not that much to it! Although he had heard about God and listened to the stories, Bert's faith comes from a very real knowledge of God in his life, hey, God wants this to get personal! So where did this belief come from, how did he decide he wanted to become a Christian?

> I had a fantastic teacher when I was in primary school who made the gospel stories come alive, really made them relevant to me even at that age. I used to look forward to Mondays when he would teach us and I used to get such a great feeling inside when he spoke about God. He really connected with me and that was a big turning point. It made me start to ask questions and from that point on I knew I believed in God and that He was real to me.

Apart from *feeling* you want to be a Christian, how do we get personal with God, how do we begin to let Him have a relationship with us?

> I think a relationship begins when you simply talk to Him. At the end of every day, or at the beginning, just imagine Him like your dad, talk to Him in prayer like any conversation. Come to Him and you can discuss anything; your day, problems, school, job, anything, just take it to God in prayer. He is there and He wants to hear from us. I just imagine someone like my father, but God is our Heavenly Father, more special, He is the Big Man, the King.

The Big Man? Excellent, God just wants us to come to Him like we would any of our friends. We can sometimes have a distorted image of God if our earthly mum or dad has been lacking in parental skills! However, it can help us to realise God is like the very best, most trustworthy, genuine, there-for-you mate ever. Basically He is love. So, becoming a Christian was a huge thing to Bert, changing his life. Sometimes we get taught a little about Christianity at school or some of us go to church and know the stories. What do you actually need to do once you have decided to go for it, how do you become a Christian, is there a ceremony?

There is no ceremony! You just do it for yourself. I simply prayed, asking Jesus into my life, asking him to forgive everything I'd done wrong and making him number one. Perhaps some of your friends and family will notice a difference in you, and as you start to read your Bible every day, pray when you get up in the morning and last thing at night, God certainly brings about change. In your normal life you should be trying to live according to the Bible, but that is so difficult and, of course, we make mistakes and sin but we only need to ask Him for forgiveness and keep on trying. There is no need for a big ceremony, just come to know God in your life, that's what's important.

Phew, that's a bit of a relief, no public ceremony that results in a tattoo on your forehead! So, we ask God into our lives and hey presto, we're changed, we're different! How? Well God doesn't ask us to go it alone, from the moment we ask Him into our lives – He sends some assistance – His helper, known as His Holy Spirit. Sounds a bit off the wall – Holy what? Who is this Spirit and does he bring His own toothbrush?!

It's different for every believer, but I know when I became filled with His Spirit He gave me tremendous support. I know His Spirit is within me now, I can actually feel Him at times. I feel like I am much closer to God and that He is working in me. I think He guides me, He comes to remind me of what's important, for example, if I am about to lose my temper over something trivial He seems to be there. These trivial things aren't important, it's God that's important. His Spirit also brings power, enables you to stand with people who don't believe and talk easily about your faith. That's His Spirit.

Hey, a Holy Spirit who brings you courage and keeps you on track, puts *Casper* in the shade! Life for Bert has been a bit of a rollercoaster at times, but from an early age he believed in the Lord, wow! He took lots of criticism from the press in Scotland when he first arrived, becoming the scapegoat for Rangers' slump in form. Surely if he has been a Christian for a long time his life should have been very easy, no hassle at all, after all, isn't being a Christian supposed to make everything good?

> Absolutely not, you know how the world is, full of crime, war and trouble. Adam and Eve blew it in paradise and we would have done the same. That's why there's lots of pain and sorrow in this world because human beings do a lot of stupid things. With the help of God we can survive it and be saved. We as Christians don't escape the bad times but with Him we come through them.

So, there are no guarantees we will have an easy life, but there are plenty of guarantees we will have eternity spent in absolute heaven where we'll meet our God, our creator, the most mighty, extraordinary, mind blowing, holy, King of kings which is well worth hanging in for and looking forward to. Another thing about being a Christian that seems an impossible task is our attitude to others. Do we really need to be turning the other cheek, seriously forgiving *everyone*, surely God doesn't want us to put up with criticism or injustice, after all, wouldn't Bert have liked to 'spit the dummy' at the press who attacked him?

> I've said a few things in discussion, but I've never sworn or lost my temper, that's not my way. I just have to give the whole press situation up to God. I hope that they'll see the light one day, realise what it's all about, but it was hard at times. I'm not easily upset by traffic jams, rudeness or trivial things, I keep reminding myself that these things aren't really important. God is what's important and I have to get on and play my football. When you consider things like cancer, war and poverty, I want to thank God that my life is as good as it is. I have so much, my family are well and beautiful, little things are not important.

My cheek is turned; say what you like about my book! So if we come to accept that Jesus is our Lord and Saviour, how does that change us? Does the fact that we want to have Christ in our lives mean we have to stop having fun and become all hell, fire and brimstone, never smiling again? After all we can look around and find Christians who look like they have received anything but good news! So how does Bert think being a Christian has shaped him and does he still have fun?

> I come from a really strict religious upbringing, very serious. We used to walk to church on Sundays, read the Bible, no television, no tabloids, etc, but sometimes I think they just concentrated on the gloomy things, looked for the negative and I did wonder if they had found happiness. However, you have to be joyful when you know God has put everything in perspective. We know there is life after this miserable one, we should be happy that in the midst of life's stresses, we have God, we have His sunshine. Not all footballers are as we're portrayed in the media, we have a bad image. I can still go out and enjoy myself with the boys or friends, I like nice restaurants, enjoy a glass of wine, but I am always following God not the world. We are not boring just because we are Christians!

Amen to that! Bert was not always going to be a footballer; he originally set out to study PE at college. However, when he was a teenager it became apparent he was actually quite good on the pitch (bit of an understatement there!). So when did he think he might be good enough to do this professionally and does he believe God is in his career?

> God helped me to become a professional, it was never in my mind. I didn't really think I was good enough; I actually wanted to be a park ranger or a PE teacher. When I was 17 the manager said I should be in the first team squad, offered me a contract (which seemed a fortune to me then!) and I began to play in the team. I still continued with my PE studies until I was 21.

Hooray, being a Christian doesn't mean we have to give up on our dreams to succeed, in fact, He can lead us to success and to happiness. I like this God! We may have come to the view that there really is a God, we do believe and we really do want to know Him better, after all, there are to be people everywhere who talk about 'having a relationship' with Him. Isn't that hard when He's invisible? How does Bert have a relationship with Him?

> We need to imagine Him as a real person, someone we love, but it can be very difficult. We need to keep talking to Him, keep praying, we need to get close to really feel Him in our lives and that can seem strange when we are talking about someone we can't even see. God wants us to know Him better, to be in every moment, so I try to see Him like my father and trust Him with my prayers. The relationship becomes even stronger because He answers them. The whole three-in-one thing, Father, Son and Holy Spirit is confusing but God can help us to understand.

He helps us to understand, that's good. The three-in-one thing Bert refers to is otherwise known as the Trinity, God in three persons, God the Father, Jesus the Son and the Holy Spirit, eh, what? How would Bert explain this, are all three invisible persons different?

> God is for me the main person, the creator, without God there would not have been a Son. Jesus, God's son, became one of us, lived a life like all of us, but could resist the world with all its sins and bad pleasures. That's why He could die for us and rise again, to save our lives. The Holy Spirit is the helpline or lifeline to God. He is always there for immediate help in our lives and he strengthens our faith. Fantastic, all three parts make God so powerful. That's why He is the only one.

Excellent, God has made Himself available and accessible to us in three different ways: all connected, all powerful, all for us, all God, wow! It's often pictured like an egg. One single thing, yet three separate parts; the yolk, white and shell, simple really. So for Bert and for so many of us God can really be *all* things to all people. He is this divine person, Lord of all, yet He became human, one of us, and suffered torture, cruelty, rejection, pain and sorrow all so that we could be saved and really know Him. If that's not enough, after He rose again to heaven He sent His Spirit, His presence, to come and live in us, keep us close to Him to lead us and direct us. Now that really is awesome. God, we are totally full of respect! Sometimes the more we try and understand the Trinity the more we understand the mystery of God. He is awesome, majestic, creator of everything, yet He lives right in your heart. So, we start to pray more, read our Bibles and talk to others, how does Bert think God wants us to know Him? How can we open our lives up to Him, really let Him in?

> I just make room and time for Him every day. God answers me in the way my family has health or through my football career, and that encourages me. Each time I come to God through the Bible or prayer, I feel good and I come to know Him better so I want to tell Him everything.

Okay, we're on our Christian walk now, we're having a relationship with God, what do we do if it feels like we aren't actually going anywhere? We're talking to the Lord and quite frankly we think we are boring Him because it doesn't appear He is listening to us. What do you do when this Christianity, which you are trying hard to get into, seems to be happening for others but all you're getting is zilch?

> Patience, we need to persevere. I am fortunate with the way my life is going, but I know it is not like that for everyone. My advice would be just keep going. If it seems your prayers aren't being answered, don't give up. You have to grow in your faith but you will win in the end. God hears everything you ask for and sees every time you read your Bible. He wants the best for you too, you just need to concentrate on the little things that are good in your life at the moment and trust He'll bring you the big things. He does love you. God can change situations, turn things around, and He does have good plans for us. We need to keep turning to Him.

Here is something that is really confusing, how do we know what we believe is right? Some people believe Muslims worship the same God with a different name, Hinduism is real to Hindus, Buddhists are kind and gentle, so how do we know our God is the only one?

> This is such a difficult one, but it is proven historically that

biblical events happened. Jesus definitely lived, He was crucified and He did rise again, the empty tomb was there. It's also a feeling, something we know. God answers our prayers, sent His son, gave us life, these things are difficult to prove or explain that's why it is called faith. However, I know when I come to Him, He is real. He tells us in His word He is the only God and everything else is a false idol we are not to worship. I believe and know that to be true.

Perhaps we need to be telling other people about this, hey, that could be another chapter! It does seem as we look around the world that religion plays a part in an awful lot of grief that's happening. Surely being a Christian is all about love and forgiveness, how can we make sure that our faith is something good and pure and not something dodgy, how can we stop Christianity having a bad name?

I know people blame religion for much of the trouble in the world, especially places such as Northern Ireland or Yugoslavia, but I don't believe these wars were about God, they were about land. God did not create war, He tries to stop it. Christianity is something beautiful and that's what people should know. The truth about God is all good news and we have to get that message across. He did not create these troubles.

Bert is involved in a game where people are keen to offer advice, like 'get a move on', 'pass it over here', 'tackle', 'shoot', 'move', etc (and that's just the advice we can print!). He was a player at a high profile club; did being a Christian make a difference in the workplace and did he feel under pressure to be good?

I didn't feel any pressure at all, certainly not from my team mates. Sometimes they made a joke about it, but I believe they also thought about what it is I believe. Footballers have a tough guy image but that's not always true. I'm always asked if I should be tackling hard, elbowing people and I have to say that that is not in my nature anyway. Football is a physical game and sometimes these things happen, but we are all professionals and respect each other off the field, even Rangers and Celtic players! It doesn't harm my relationship with God, He has blessed my football. There's not more pressure on me because my career is higher profile, I just need to keep turning to Him.

Life as a Christian may not be trouble free, but it does come with the guarantee that Jesus is always by your side and His spirit lives within you, guiding you. So, perhaps we face hassle in relationships, with a teacher, employer, mate, whoever, as a Christian we have someone to talk to who is wise, powerful and awesome. I'm glad His name is Jesus and He's on my side! We know we worship the one true God, we know He loves us and wants the best for us; we know He has plans for us, what now?

How do we actually keep this faith alive, keep it going all through life until heaven? It does seem quite a long way off.

I keep on praying and so does my wife. We read the Bible together along with our kids and always look to Him for I need God to support me every day.

I also think church is important to help you keep going, it gives you a good feeling as you meet other people who are trying to find Him or who believe the same as you.

Talking with other Christians helps. We need to encourage one another but most importantly we need to keep on turning to Him and giving Him our whole lives.

Aha, it's that simple, accept Him into your life, give Him your heart and He will give you His! I like the idea of trusting my heart to the creator of the universe who knows each and every hair on my head. Every day of my life, even before I was born, He loves me more than I could ever begin to imagine, He loves justice and truth. Hey, sounds a lot more trustworthy and powerful than the things I worshipped before!

I am a Christian, now that sounds good!

Further Scripture reading

Acts 4 v4
But many who heard the message believed and the number of men grew to about five thousand.

John 1 v12
Yet to all those who received Him, to those who believed in His name, He gave the right to become children of God...

John 3 v16
For God so loved the world that He gave His one and only Son, that whoever believes in Him shall not perish, but have eternal life.

Acts 10 v42
All the prophets testify about Him that everyone who believes in Him receives forgiveness of sin through His Name.

Acts 4 v12
Salvation is found in no-one else, for there is no other name under heaven given to men by which we must be saved.

Juan Carlos Valeron

DATE OF BIRTH: 17.06.74

POSITION: Midfielder

CLUB HISTORY: Arguinegin, Las Palmas, Mallorca, Atletico Madrid, Deportivo La Coruna

INTERNATIONAL HISTORY: Full caps for Spain

FAVOURITE ALL-TIME FOOTBALL ELEVEN (*4/4/2 formation*):
I have only selected those I've seen playing.

		Taffarel		
Cafu	Baresi		Maldini	Roberto Carlos
Zidane	Guardiola		Laudrup M	Maradona
	Van Basten		Romario	

FAVOURITE PIECE OF SCRIPTURE: **Psalm 23**

Juan Carlos Valeron
God loves everyone – even you!

So, God says repeatedly in the Bible how much He loves us, how much He delights in us, how special we are, great. Does He really mean *you* though, you know, even though you aren't exactly perfect, in fact quite far from it at times. It can be difficult to really get a handle on this great love, especially if you haven't had a lot of it in your life. God loves us in a very different way from anyone else; He loves us with a perfect love, a love that has no end. Some people are blessed with excellent parents who do a good job of bringing them up, of loving them, caring for them and making them secure, but even this is short of what God has in store for us. Some people have had little love in their lives to date, for a variety of reasons, perhaps with parents or family who have not loved them unconditionally. God wants to help you. He loves you in a way that is so big it takes your breath away. God wants you to know that you are so special to Him, He sent His only Son, Jesus, to die on the cross for you, yep, for you.

God doesn't just love us when we are trusting and obeying Him, following His way (although it's so much better for us when we do!), nope, He loves us even when we are going astray. He longs for us to turn back to Him. One person who is convinced that God loves us all unconditionally is Spanish sensation, Juan Carlos Valeron, a Christian now for over 20 years.

I have believed in God since I was a very small boy. When I became a teenager I came to know God in a very personal way, He became real to me as did His great love.

So even teenagers are loved by God, *excellent*! Seems God can speak to us at any age or stage, perhaps it's us who don't listen. Is God speaking to you, do you have a relationship with Him? Perhaps it's time to stop rejecting His offers and promises and just accept them. Juan Carlos is an exciting footballer to watch with an abundance of talent and flair, another annoyingly nice guy then! So perhaps it's easy for him to love God, perhaps it's easy for God to care for Juan and speak to him. Would he still believe God loves us all if he knew what we did last week? How does Juan Carlos accept that God loves us all not just a select few who live a good life and are devoted to Jesus? Where does he get the idea that God loves us all, even us less loveable, moody ones who struggle with life in general?

The very fact that He created us and gave us life.

God already knew you before you were formed and He loves you, He didn't make some to love and others to reject. He has the power over everything in creation, He chose to make you and He knows everything about you. The Bible tells us that God so loved the world, not just part of it, that He sent Jesus. It seems unlikely that you, however miserable you think you are, would be the only person in the world God didn't love! So, it's not up to us then, God just loves us. Some of us can have a very human view of love, believing it's something we have to earn or work for, sometimes even compete for. Even those lucky enough to have great parents still have a slightly imperfect view of love, just because parents are human and not perfect. God however IS perfect and so is His love, so how do we begin to understand it, what is perfect love? How does Juan Carlos explain this great and awesome love God has for us.

He gave His own Son Jesus with love to us!

If you really think about that, let it truly sink in, that this God who created all of us, one by one, was so desperate to see us saved, He sent Jesus to die for us, that really shows true love. God has shown time and time again by the life and ministry of Jesus what exactly perfect love is, to put Him first in everything and to love one another as we love ourselves. Jesus was the perfect example of God's love for us. Perfect love might not be everywhere in our daily lives with family and friends, but it is on offer 24/7 from our Father in heaven, the same God who forgives every screw-up and mistake if you're truly sorry. I like the sound of this God more and more. Juan Carlos has been blessed with a wonderful talent on the pitch and has played in some pretty impressive fixtures, alongside some pretty impressive teammates. So does he see his talent as an example of God's love, a gift to him from his Heavenly Father?

Yes, absolutely, I think my talent at football is a gift from God for me to enjoy.

Football is what Juan Carlos likes doing, has a passion for and God tells us He longs to give us the desires of our hearts. Why would God give us a gift we didn't enjoy? Juan Carlos is blessed to play a sport he loves and is good at while still realising it's all just temporary. God has given him the opportunity to play football because He loves him and He wants to bless all of His children. Even you! So, God might actually have given you the chance to shine at something you enjoy doing, hmmm, not such a bad gift giver after all. Football, as I keep moaning about, isn't everyone's talent, however, when you do find something you are talented at or enjoy doing consider that it might actually have come from God, a sign of His love, and you might just want to give thanks for it! So when we consider all the blessings God has given us, our health, our families, our dreams, our freedom, it becomes clearer how much He loves us. For some life has been a series of disappointments so far, perhaps losing a parent, being bullied, overcoming a disability, not to mention those who are abused or starving, how does Juan Carlos explain God's love in difficult circumstances? If God loves us all why are some people's circumstances so much better than others?

In lots of situations people aren't always guilty of anything. Sometimes though, it's the consequences of years of sin.

We sometimes reap the sorrows of years of sinning, staying away from God's will and just doing things our own way. He doesn't send grief and heartache to us, but we often have to suffer it. However we're never alone as God promises to be with us in the midst of everything. That's how much He loves us. So even in the midst of trials and heartache, God is there, hurting with us. Love can be seen and demonstrated between two people or more in a variety of ways. We all know the embarrassing displays of affection couples display when they are full of love and romance, and parents can show their love by hugs, gifts, discipline(!), nursing, listening, driving and generally being there, while our mates just seem to say the right thing or be there when we need them, but how does God show His great love for us?

God shows His love in the life of Jesus, His death for us and the blessings that we see each day.

All around us are the signs of Gods love, of His many blessings. He created such beauty and joy on our earth and in our lives, but sometimes we are too busy to notice or we concentrate on the mess man has made of it. Organisations that look after our environment are so vital, such as Greenpeace or La Rocha, perhaps God has given you a passion to preserve our earth, get involved! I will take extra notice of the sunsets and beaches from now on!

Other signs of God's love for us can be the people He brings into our lives. Friends can be such a blessing, as can families (well, at birthdays anyway!) and it never ceases to amaze me how, since I gave my life to Christ, He puts the right people in the right place at the right time. God's love for us often remains unseen or unnoticed, but I'm sure when we get to Heaven we will understand how many times His almighty hand worked in our lives to save us from danger or harm, and to keep us on track. That's love, when you don't even want recognition for protecting and helping a person who constantly ignores you, moans about you or even refuses to believe you exist!

God has a plan for each and every one of us, yet we often stray far from where He wants us to be. What does it mean then when we are off the track, when we are following the world's ways, not the Bible's, does God stop loving us then? Well, He might not love what we are doing or saying, but He wants us to get back on track, to turn back to Him and ask for His forgiveness and grace. God hates sin, not the sinner. Whew, let's just get this straight, He keeps on loving us even when we are sinning? *Wow!* Aha, maybe He just means He would *like* to love us; maybe if we are sinning He turns His back on us. Surely Juan Carlos doesn't believe that no matter what we do, no matter how bad we are God continues to love us?

Yes, that's what I believe!

So, His love is perfect and He longs for a relationship with His children. Jesus came and ministered to some of the real outcasts of the day, people who were sinners, yet He wanted to share that love of God with them. Why wouldn't it be the same today, after all, God is a God of love, He might even love teenagers. Awesome! However much we are told that God's love is forever sometimes it doesn't *feel* like it. Sometimes we listen to the enemy and when we have sinned, whether it's something bad we have been thinking about, or if we know our attitude stinks, or we have ignored some one who needs us, made a fool of people we don't really like, *whatever*, we can't feel God's love in our lives. That's when it's a good idea to come closer to God whatever way you can. Church is important, as is praying, praising, fellowship, all the things that bring you back into a relationship with Him. Reading your Bible is so important because that's God's word to you and you realise it's not about how you *feel*, the *fact* is God loves you! So prayer and praise are actually quite essential in this walk with God! We already know that God is with us 24/7 and much as church is important and necessary for our spiritual growth, we know that we don't need to be in a special building to worship Him, just give Him your heart, words, mind and body wherever you are then watch your attitude change as He gives His love to you, regardless of your *feelings*! God is not likely to take away His love just because we sin, but often we take ourselves away from His blessings WHEN we are sinning. Getting drunk and high at the party may seem like a great idea at the time, but as we lie in a corner vomiting, or worse, spend the night in a cell or in a strange flat, we often take ourselves out of the place God had intended our blessing to be, woops, not quite so appealing, missing our destiny due to a hangover! Juan Carlos grew up in a land of sea, sun and sand, with a talent to professionally play the game he loves – how blessed! With a life like that, perhaps it's easier to say God loves everyone and that we are all blessed. Does he believe though, that sometimes, God gets angry with humans and He shows this on earth?

> God teaches us in the Bible that He sometimes gets angry about sin. Jesus Himself intercedes for us when we do things badly, teaches us the right way.

How fabulous is that, if we make mistakes and get into dodgy things Jesus is on hand to plead for us, to state our case and to pay the price – humbling or what? He has set a way for us to live our lives and He knows that we are only going to hurt ourselves when we ignore Him and do our own thing. Perhaps when our parents, friends or relatives seem to be on our case, it's not that they don't understand us – it's maybe that we don't understand how much they love us. After all it would be a pretty poor parent who just ignored the fact their child was on the path to self-destruction! God may have enough love to hug the world and back again, but does He expect us to do the same? Are we, as Christians, expected to love our neighbours, whatever, even when they are really annoying?

> Yes, it's a command of Jesus, pure and simple.

Okay, Juan Carlos suggests we love our neighbour then! Life would be pretty dull, we are often informed, if we were all the same (but not if we looked like Orlando or Beyonce!). Well, loving your neighbour may mean putting up with things unfamiliar or new to you, but you should never compromise your beliefs. Loving people who are confused or sinning might mean pointing them in God's direction. Loving someone who is taunting you, ignoring you, lying about you might be hard (try nearly impossible), but with a deep breath, lots of prayer and a smattering of God's love in your life and in your heart, you can act with love even when you don't feel like it! Go on, give it a try, grit your teeth and smile, say 'No problem' instead of 'Do it yourself'! Let's get our heads round that one then; God wants US to love everyone too! We have been accepted and forgiven, cleansed and saved all because of the life, death and resurrection of Jesus. We need to appreciate just exactly how huge that is, can you imagine watching the one you love suffer and die while you turn away, just so that the ones who ignore you and disobey you can be saved, now that's love! How does Juan Carlos get his head round this, how do we begin to understand the ultimate sacrifice?

> It's difficult to understand the sacrifice of Christ, simply accept it. It's something so large, although when you know God personally you can understand it some of the way.

Aha, it's so incredible that it blows you away, its awesome. We can't fully understand it but we can accept it, accept the sacrifice God has made. Once you have a relationship with Jesus, although His crucifixion is still huge, your relationship with Him makes it a little easier to understand. So far this great love thing between God and us is very one-sided, we get, we receive and we take, but how do we *give*, how do we return this great love to God?

> We can return His love by trying to do His will and we should also enjoy all the different blessings He has given us.

So, a little bit of worship and gratitude wouldn't go amiss, it's a two-way thing after all! Jesus paid the price for all of our sins, all of our mistakes, and all He wants in return is our hearts and our love, seems a fair exchange to me. Oh yeah and we get eternal peace and happiness in the presence of our Lord!

He gives us love and peace, but we often choose to ignore Him and do it our own way, with tragic results. God is so much more than our judge and lawgiver, He is LOVE, pure and simple.

Football is a sport loved by many as Juan Carlos experiences in every game, so how does he cope with this love, doesn't he ever worry he will love it too much, give it too much of his time, after all, how would he cope if the football stopped? Can we love earthly things too much?

Football for me is one of the many things God has given us to enjoy, but we should not put it above God.

It's important that we always put the God who made us first, who gave us these gifts and that we don't put things like football ahead of Him. We must always worship our God, the creator, nothing else. Sounds simple, 'Love the Lord your God above all else, and worship no false idols', hmmm, perhaps some of us need to work on that one! Juan Carlos seems to have learned the very important truth, God loves him no matter what, he cannot earn it, he cannot it buy it, he cannot lose it, he just enjoys it. What advice would he give those who are struggling with this, who can't seem to accept it and still feel unworthy?

The best I can do is share my example, speak of what God has done for me and in my life.

God loves you and it's so important that you know that, and live like you know it. You are special to Him. Live your life for Him, telling others of your experiences and life with faith. If you're struggling to find this God, His love or power, then read the Bible, books like this, go to a church, listen to ordinary people, young and old, fit or not, as they tell you how knowing Jesus has changed their lives. Then believe He wants to do the same for you. God doesn't want you to try to impress Him, He just wants you to accept His free love and trust Him, for He will never let you down or hurt you, God is love. If we accept the Bible as God's Word, where does it speak most to Juan Carlos of God's love, how does the Bible convince him he believes in a God of love?

That all depends on the moment. Sometimes it can be a very particular verse or passage that God uses to speak to me, the next day another. Sometimes a verse we have read before can seem completely new to us. God can use the whole Bible to speak of His love, after all, it's His Word.

There you go then, the Bible is full of examples and stories of God's unfailing love for you – just open it and accept. So, when you have read this entire chapter and consider the career of Juan Carlos, it seems to me that he is indeed blessed and certainly getting something right. Juan Carlos and everyone in this book are living life according to the will and word of an invisible God, unseen, yes, but not unreachable and when you consider **John 3 v16** where it says: *For God so loved the world that he gave his one and only Son, that whoever believes in him shall not perish but have eternal life.* It makes you think, *God loves you*, yes even *you*! Ready to accept and enjoy it?

Further Scripture reading

Romans 5 v8
But God demonstrates His own love for us in this: While we were still sinners, Christ died for us.

Romans 8 vs38–39
For I am convinced that neither death nor life, angels nor demons, neither the present nor the future, nor any powers, neither height nor depth, nor anything else in all creation, will be able to separate us from the love of God that is in Christ Jesus our Lord.

1 John 4 v16
God is love. Whoever lives in love lives in God, and God in him.

Marvin Andrews

DATE OF BIRTH: 22.12.75

POSITION: Defender

CLUB HISTORY: Motown F.C, Carib F.C, Raith Rovers, Livingston, Rangers

INTERNATIONAL HISTORY: Full caps for Trinidad and Tobago

BEST EVER FOOTBALL MOMENT: Scoring the first goal in the 2002 World Cup Qualifiers.

BEST EVER SPIRITUAL MOMENT: Being born again.

FAVOURITE ALL-TIME FOOTBALL ELEVEN (*4/4/2 formation*):

Canazaries			
Maldini	Staam	Baresi	Roberto Carlos
Ronaldinho	Zidane	Maradona	Kaka
Pele		Romario	

FAVOURITE PIECE OF SCRIPTURE:
Luke 1 v37 *For nothing is impossible with God.*

Marvin Andrews
The power of prayer

By this stage in our walk with God we are looking pretty good for eternal life, we're totally cool about being a Christian (and we didn't need a tank top!), we're happy to find out more about God, in fact, he wants a relationship with us. Eh, how could that happen given he's invisible and not at the end of a phone? This chapter should help us because it's about prayer, apparently one of the most important ways we communicate with God. People tell God a lot of things through prayer, should we? One person who thinks so is Marvin Andrews, defender with Rangers Football Club and Trinidad and Tobago. He has been a Christian for many years now and is convinced prayer is a huge part of his Christian walk. So if it's so important Marvin, how do we do it?

> You speak to God just exactly the same way you speak to friends or family except you can't see Him. You can find a quiet place and talk to Him just as if He were right there beside you. He says in the Bible any time you pray, wherever you are, He can hear you whenever you call upon Him. You can be sitting down, kneeling, lying on your bed, whatever you prefer, just have a conversation with God like you do with your friends.

Marvin came from a very poor background on the sun-kissed Caribbean island of Trinidad and his life could have been so very different. Although his family often went to church he was not a true believer. However, Marvin knows that even though he wasn't giving his life fully to God he still knew the Lord was there. So why did Marvin go from occasionally reading his Bible and going to church to having his incredible, unshakeable faith?

> I was very ill with osteitis pubis, a painful lower abdominal injury. I didn't have any hope as the doctors told me I needed surgery and might not be able to play again. I turned to God and along with my minister, Joe Nwokoye, I prayed morning, noon and night for His healing. He healed me miraculously, without surgery, and from that moment on I trusted in Him and gave Him my life. After all if he can heal an injury the doctors said I couldn't recover from, what else can He do?

Marvin then found a good church and began to trust the Lord in every area of his life. How did his prayer life increase with this new faith?

> The more I got to know God, the more my prayer life increased. I realised it wasn't just my injury He could heal but, through prayer, God could bring change to all the problems in my life. I started to ask God for greater things, to help me with all I wanted to achieve in life and I saw that the only way was to pray. I pray three times a day, every day, and now it's part of my life like brushing my teeth or having a shower.

Presuming we shower and brush our teeth regularly!

While at Livingstone, Marvin was featured a lot in the Scottish press, famously turning down a chance to join Dundee United, another club in the Scottish Premier League, because the Lord told him not to go there, eh?

> When I heard Dundee United wanted to sign me I just prayed God would give me guidance. Although they were a bigger club and Livingston had financial difficulties at the time I only wanted to go where God told me to. I prayed really hard about it, went to bed that night, then the next morning as I read my Word for the day, God told me to stay at Livingston for the moment. So that's exactly what I did. I stayed and that season we won the CIS Cup, I know it was God's Will.

So after his daily Bible reading Martin was convinced God wanted him to stay put – wow!

Marvin's decision to trust God and go against the advice of the 'world' (the press and most of Scottish football) was proven a wise one when in the summer of 2004 Rangers, one of the top two clubs in the country, made a bid for him and brought him to Ibrox – now that's a real blessing! How did Marvin get guidance this time, was the fact they were a top club a pointer?

It was exactly the same as before, I prayed for guidance, listened to His word and obeyed.

Although Rangers are a much bigger club I wanted to be sure God wanted me to go, which He did. In everything I do, I consult God first through prayer.

Does Marvin pray about football results? Is it okay to ask God for specific things?

You can ask God for whatever you want, He says in **Matthew 7 v7** Ask and it will be given to you; seek and you will find; knock and the door will be opened to you. The only reason God doesn't answer is if you ask with the wrong motives. If you ask for someone who has angered you to be harmed or for great wealth with which you would be greedy, He won't grant these, but anything that you need or desire you can ask Him for.

This prayer lark is really quite awesome, after all, you are able to communicate with the creator of the universe without an appointment, not bad. When we come to God in prayer is it supposed to be on our knees where we stay for hours? After all, sometimes you just need a quick chat, a little reassurance or something small, and on our knees isn't exactly comfortable for long!

You can come for a chat when you are on your knees, standing up, lying down, in the bathroom, whatever. Wherever you call upon God, He is there. When you are in the shower instead of singing you can pray. There is no special position, you don't need to have your hands clasped or anything like that. The Bible tells you not to be like the Pharisees, praying for hours to impress other people, but just pray when you can. He will answer prayers that last for just a split second, He will also answer prayers that last a while, it's just important to come to Him.

Communicating with God would seem to be a very big part of who Marvin is, the guy seems to be in constant touch with Jesus. That's encouraging, but what can sometimes be a little confusing is how do we know God has heard our concerns or requests? After all we don't tell the doctor all our symptoms then walk out the door before he diagnoses us, how do we get a reply from God?

From our friends, family, books, but most of all through the Bible, that's the most frequent way He speaks to us. God also speaks through dreams, through a message on a wall or even on someone's tee-shirt. Sometimes we are waiting for a big powerful voice but just listen for that still, small voice. He speaks to you through your heart and it's not loud and booming. Another way He can speak is through your thoughts, for example if you pray for direction and something immediately pops into your head that's how God can speak to you.

We need to be sensitive to all things around about us because God can use all things to speak to us, even our enemies.

Yikes, even our enemies, wait a minute, how do we know it's from God? What if it's just someone taking the mickey?

If something is from God, you will know. When you hear from God you have peace, if you don't have peace with what is said then it's not from Him.

Hearing from our Heavenly Father can be the most amazing thing. To know that He is listening and wants to give us our hearts desires is mindblowing, after all He does have a universe to run! Marvin has seen a lot of doors open because of his football, a lot of opportunities to share his faith and to tell other people about Jesus.

Is this something he prays about, does he meet people just by chance, or does Marvin pray for opportunities and for guidance?

> I pray for opportunities and that He may open doors for me to share the gospel with as many people as possible. There are so many people who are depressed and under the schemes of the devil and this is something I have really prayed about. He has blessed me by opening so many doors into schools, churches, football teams, etc just so I can meet different people and tell them about His truth. God is a respecter of all people and I pray He gives me many opportunities to tell them about Him and that He gives me wisdom when I am with them. This book is an opportunity to share the gospel and tell others about His love and I have prayed about this too, basically I just keep on praying to be used by God to see people saved after all that's the most important thing about my faith, God wants to see *all* His children saved.

Marvin enjoys church and his Bible, but you sense that for him his prayer life is one of the most vital ways to keep in touch with God. So is there a set time he prays, should we be coming to God as if by appointment each day or is it just when and if you want?

> With God, any time is a good time, He is always listening. You can say you will fit God into your timetable, for example, prayers at 6 pm but the devil can come and make sure you are busy then therefore you should pray when you can. The devil comes to steal, kill and destroy, and he doesn't want us to pray so he will do whatever he can to stop us.

> Setting times are fine, but so is just chatting to God in prayer whenever you can.

For most of us praying is something that takes time and practice. I'm sure God is glad each time we pray, but delighted when we actually get round to telling Him exactly what's in our hearts.

Rangers Football Club is a huge organization, the team regularly plays in front of over 50 000 spectators, and with supporters having his name adorning thousands of shirts it's a massive responsibility.

So, how does he stay grounded, how does he cope with this fame and adoration?

> Prayer helps, I just need to obey God. I confess the Word of God through prayer. The Bible says God will exalt the humble and I try to be humble in everything I do. I know that anything I achieve is down to Him, I'm not the one responsible. All the success in my life is not because of any talent I have or anything about me, its all about the Lord Jesus and what He is doing for me.

Oops, kinda makes the swollen head at the end of a good game of FIFA 2005 disappear!

Rangers and Celtic are two clubs in Glasgow with a sad history of sectarianism, a hatred of each other loosely based on the Protestant/Catholic divide, so how does Marvin pray into this situation?

> I pray everyday that God will love both sides, that He will touch them. What they do and what they fight about is nothing to do with God; He is love. I pray that they will be moved by Him to seek the ways of God, not these ways.

Marvin trusts in this God of love and power. How does he trust that God is interested in everything that we are, such as what to wear to a party or science homework?

> He is interested in the little details which are concerned with right or wrong. He is bothered about whether you do your homework or study because He knows you need to work hard to learn and succeed. He is also concerned with the way you speak to your parents or elders, He doesn't want you to be cheeky to them or speak back to them. He doesn't want you to pick up stones and smash windows. He isn't concerned if you want to have your hair long or short, dyed or not, He isn't concerned with what kind of trainers or jeans you wear, if you ride a skateboard or a bike, what clothes you wear, these are choices He gave all of us. God wants us to do the good things however small they seem and He doesn't want us to do the bad

things however small they may seem. If you have any problems you should come to God. He tells us not to worry, He is there for everything.

Our prayer life is obviously a big part of who we are as Christians and it's something which Marvin takes seriously, so how does he cope when it seems God is not answering our prayers and the circumstances don't seem to be changing?

> You continue praying. God is the God who answers everything. He may allow you to wait, not get it right away, but He will provide when He knows you are in need. After all, if you ask for a car aged 13 He won't answer, but when you're 17 and old enough to drive, he will. God tells us He will answer all who call on Him but you have to believe. You have to trust that God will answer your prayer. If you have asked God for new trainers and they aren't here yet, keep on asking. Take everything to Him in prayer and persevere.

God is obviously a lot bigger and more powerful than us (we didn't part the Red Sea!), yet He is also very close and personal, thank goodness. Marvin has been a good friend in Christ to many people and one way he believes God wants us to be there for our mates is to pray for them. What, shift the goalposts from us to others, is that the way?

> We should always pray for others, as God wants the whole world to be saved. Scripture says in **1 Timothy 2 v1** *I urge, then, first of all, that requests, prayers, intercession and thanksgiving be made for everyone.* After all if He has answered our prayers, why wouldn't we want to pray for our sisters or brothers or parents or friends?

The language of our prayer is simple, It's just a conversation, albeit with the Lord God Almighty! We now know that He wants us to pray for others, sorted. However, God has so many plans for us, so many good things to deliver, that He delights in us coming together to give thanks, uh, does that mean He wants us to pray with others as well? Out loud?

It says in **Matthew 18 vs19–20** *Again, I tell you that if two of you on earth agree about anything you ask for, it will be done for you by my Father in heaven. For where two or three come together in my name, there am I with them.* God is a God who loves unity, He wants you to combine together as one and become stronger. The devil hates to see unity because he knows the power of people praying together. It is good to come with others and pray, you can encourage one another by your prayers.

> Our prayer life can be a fantastic means of chatting with God and certainly beneficial to us as His children, so now we simply need to make some space and get talking, let God know how much we need and love Him.

Wait a minute though, what if we're in a dark place, unable to see anything good in our lives, does God really want to hear from us, hear our ranting, or should we only go to God with good things, our thanks or requests?

> God doesn't want us to come to him while we are still angry and bothered, He tells us to go and forgive that person, then come to Him to pray. It's not that he doesn't want to hear from us, but He knows if we are thinking evil thoughts then we cannot concentrate on Him and receive His peace. However, we can go to God and ask Him to help us to forgive our enemies. He can help us to get rid of the anger and love them again, that's why He wants us to bring Him our needs. Problems come, certain things happen, only God alone knows why, you have to turn to Him and ask Him to give you back your peace and love. Everything that happens is not always from God but whatever the devil does God is the one who can give you protection and peace. He explains His truth in **John 10 v10** where it says: *The thief comes only to steal and kill and destroy; I have come; said Jesus, 'that they may have life, and have it to the full.* and we need to trust Him and take Him our prayers.

Sounds to me like God is really constant and reliable, the kind of mate you would want to talk to! We read a lot in the Bible ('cos we are such avid readers of the good book!) about God answering prayer in a really powerful or dramatic way. Has Marvin ever been blown away by an answer to prayer, how has God changed situations?

Obviously my healing was miraculous, but once when playing for Livingston I was running and praying to God that I'd score a goal. Before I knew it we won a corner and 'pow!', I scored from it. I couldn't believe how fast He answered. God answers every person's prayer, as long as you trust and believe.

At times, trusting in God requires a lot of patience, especially when it seems that your prayers have been pushed to the bottom of Heaven's 'To Do' pile. These times are hard yet we don't have to go through them alone. We have spoken about praying for others, but have you considered letting others pray for you? Marvin has no problem letting his friends take his requests to the Lord and he welcomes the fellowship that comes from allowing others to carry you in prayer.

Letting others pray for us is very good. We could escape injury or accident because our parents or friends have been praying, asking for God's protection. Often we can receive things we haven't even asked for just because another has been asking God for us. Look at Peter in **Acts 12 v7**, God sent an angel to free him from prison because he heard the prayers of Peter's friends. Jesus is interceding for us in heaven right now, praying that every person on earth be saved, so its obviously a good thing for others to pray for you.

From time to time you seem to be getting it just right as a Christian. You are in constant touch with your Heavenly Father, you have a great prayer-life, a friend to pray for and with and your world is a nice one, aahhhh. So, should we just sit and give thanks all day or should we get off our backsides and widen the picture, turn our attention to 'others', not just those we know but those we don't. When there is war, famine or disaster in the world, there is an obvious prayer need, but how do we make this a regular part of our praying, how do we bring people we don't even know into our thoughts and concerns before God?

> God tells us to pray for all men. **1 Timothy 2 vs1–4** makes it clear we are to pray for everyone on this earth, we are to pray for our leaders, prime ministers and presidents. God wants to save all His children and we ought to be bringing people we don't even know before Him. We see a news report about starving children and pray for them, we don't need to know them, just lift up that situation. Wherever we see needs, such as people dying, we should be praying. When there are wars we should be praying they end quickly. God loves *all* His children, and His desire is to see them all believers, that's something we should be praying for!

Certainly enough to be going on with! Praying may seem a chore at first but it is one of the keys to freedom God gives us when we enter into a relationship with Him. Marvin is enjoying life in all its abundance. He looks set to continue to play in the top flight of Scottish Football, but more importantly for him he is sure, thanks to his daily chats with God, that he is right where God wants him to be and he is certain God gives him just the right words to speak even when being interviewed for books!

> I prayed before I answered these questions and I want you to know that everything I say and believe comes from Him. If you want to get closer to Him, it's not about Marvin Andrews or anyone else, it's all about God. Just come to Him now and every day in prayer, He loves you.

He is our Father in heaven, our daddy, and He wants us to respond to Him by loving Him, by letting Him know we are His. God is not too busy to care, and *never* too busy to listen. He is there, right in your heart, hoping you will ask him into your hopes and plans forever. Since He is the one who can give you the desires of your heart it seems pretty silly to ignore Him. And even if you don't understand the desires of your heart isn't it important to speak to the one person who does?

This chapter is now finished, I need to go and pray that you will be reading it one day!

Further Scripture reading

Matthew 6 v9

This, then, is how you should pray:
'Our Father in heaven,
hallowed be your name,
your Kingdom come,
your will be done on earth as it is in heaven.
Give us today our daily bread.
Forgive us our debts,
as we also have forgiven our debtors.
And lead us not into temptation
but deliver us from the evil one'.

Daniel 6 v10

Three times a day he got down on his knees and prayed, giving thanks to God, just as he had done before.

Ephesians 3 vs16–18

I pray that out of His glorious riches He may strengthen you with power through His Spirit in your inner being, so that Christ may dwell in your hearts through faith. And I pray that you, being rooted and established in love, may have power, together with all the saints, to grasp how wide and long and high and deep is the love of Christ, ...

Darren Moore

DATE OF BIRTH: 22.04.74

POSITION: Defender

CLUB HISTORY: Torquay, Doncaster,
Bradford, Portsmouth, West Bromwich Albion

INTERNATIONAL HISTORY: Full caps for Jamaica

BEST EVER FOOTBALL MOMENT: Scoring a goal in the last game of the season
to gain promotion to the Premiership.

BEST EVER SPIRITUAL MOMENT: Being baptised in the sea in Southsea.

FAVOURITE ALL-TIME FOOTBALL ELEVEN (*4/4/2 formation*):

		Schmeichel		
Cafu	Baresi		Maldini	Roberto Carlos
Beckham	Vierra		Keane	Zidane
	Ronaldo		Giggs	

FAVOURITE PIECE OF SCRIPTURE:
Nehemiah 8 v10 ... *the joy of the lord is your strength.*

Darren Moore
Why should we read the Bible?

O kay, as we go further into this relationship with God, in fact to GET further, reading His Word is an absolute must! That's where we can sometimes hit a problem, isn't the Bible really dead boring? Do we have to read it? For West Bromwich Albion player Darren Moore, God's Word is an absolutely vital part of his faith.

> The Bible is so vital because it's God's Word and His will for your life. No matter what you face in life, no matter what emotions you're going through, the Bible can carry you through. It's been translated for you to understand how to get through everything. It's vital for me to know how God wants me to act in my life today.

Darren Moore has been playing football since he was just a little tiddler and has reached the heights of the English Premiership, not bad for a Brummy lad. It's understandable that Christians want to get closer to the Lord and to seek His will, but how does the Bible do this; why does Darren read it?

> First and foremost you have to accept the Lord Jesus into your life, then the Holy Spirit comes to live in you. He brings you closer to Him through the Bible by using the Holy Spirit to prompt you when you are reading it. It's just like when you are at school, you have to study and meditate on something to

really get to know and understand it and it's exactly the same with the Bible. Jesus really wants to get close to us and have a relationship with us and the only way to do that is to read the Bible and for the Holy Spirit to prompt you to read certain sections; really get close to Him through His Word. Also, God tells us in **Deuteronomy 8 v3** that *man does not live on bread alone but on every word that comes from the mouth of the Lord.* This points us to reading His Word.

For many the Bible is some book that gathers dust in the corner of a spare room or is brought to church but never really read, far less understood. Isn't it written in gibberish? Is it really relevant in this modern world? Darren thinks so!

It's still very relevant to us today, after all, everything we are going through we know from the Bible that Jesus went through. He faced all the different emotions and temptations we do, all the hard times and difficulties, He has been there and lived it. One thing we can be sure of is that our Lord Jesus walked this earth for 33 years and didn't commit a single sin, that is why the Bible is still relevant, it can teach us about His life. The Bible is alive today and we need to read it and hear it.

I can't imagine living 33 hours without sinning either in thought, word or action, so this Bible which is the story of Jesus who didn't sin in 33 *years*, is certainly worth a read!

Darren Moore has enjoyed success in his footballing career, particularly in the Premiership and certainly makes use of the talents God has given him, has it always been like this? Darren may seem to have life pretty much sorted, but has he ever faced hard times, and if so, how did the Bible help?

I faced hard times, especially three years ago at Bradford City when we won promotion to the Premier League for the first time in the club's 75-year history and after playing in nearly all 57 games leading to the promotion, I was told to accept a poor contract or be sold. It was so hard as I had dreamed of playing in the Premiership since I was nine or ten, yet here I was playing in the reserves and even being subbed there. I was only a Christian for about six months and it was very difficult for me, however, I believe it was a time that God was carrying me. It says in **Nehemiah 8 v10** that *the joy of the Lord is your strength*, and that's really what sustained me, took me through, just to know that God was in this with me helped me to see it through. My fitness had gone too, but I had to cling to the verse in **Romans 8 v28** that says *God works for the good of those who love Him, who have been called according to His purpose.* Eventually Portsmouth came in for me and I went there. I had to trust in the Lord and believe in all that I read in the Bible. I've also faced injury but He brings me through because I believe He is still the healing God from Scripture. I suffered a terrible knee injury that could have kept me out of the game, but the God I read about in the Bible brought me through that too. It's not all bad times though, there has been such joy. One of the best things you can do is to accept the Lord in your life and accept He is with you in everything. When I read in the Bible of all the things people like Moses, David, Joseph and others went through, I can relate to their sufferings or hard times, but what I also see is that God never leaves them to face things alone and when they have come through they are usually changed for the better. They were blessed and that's what He does with us still.

God has certainly helped Darren find his way in life, navigating the rockier paths, but when he began reading his Bible did he know exactly where to turn to? For example, should you start at the beginning?

I started with the beginning of the New Testament, with the gospels; Matthew, Mark, Luke and John, because those four books tell us all about Jesus, everything He did for us and about His great love, after all God is Love. You can start at the beginning, Genesis, about creation and how it all began but the gospels tell you everything you need to know about our

Saviour and help us to get grounded in His word. These four give us such insights, that you can read Genesis and understand Jesus is the same God who created us. After that I bought some daily reading books and a study guide which meant I read the whole Bible in a year, a bit each day. That's the way I started and it helped me to understand His Word.

Simple then, just give God some time every day in His Word and He will do the rest! So perhaps you're on your Christian journey, following God, listening to His voice, reading His word regularly. What exactly is regularly? Do you have to spend hours using only a candle, with no food or water, poring over this book?

When it comes to reading the Bible everybody is different. I'm not saying you must spend five hours a day studying it, God understands if you can't. What I would say is if you can discipline yourself to give Him ten minutes a day and get into a quiet place, I guarantee that your understanding will increase and the revelation you get from His Word will be immense. You can't get enough of the Bible. Our desire in life should be to know His Word so well that if our Bibles were taken away we could still quote Scripture after Scripture.

Aha, so God wants you to come to His Word not out of a sense of duty or punishment, but because you want to, because you like what you read! Reading the Bible can be confusing, especially the Old Testament, lots of funny, weird names and places. The Bible may have been written a long time ago, but it's actually pretty cool once you start to get into it, it's got; fighting, love, fleeing, love, spying, love, chasing, love, stealing, love, murder, love and cool gifts – spot any themes running through it? God is undoubtedly awesome and kind and fair, so why does He want us to read about situations and circumstances that happened so long ago?

The situations that happened thousands of years ago are still happening today, that's why God wants us to read about them. There are people today who are falsely accused, have lost family members, are elated because of a job promotion or have lost everything in war or famine. God is encouraging or teaching us when we read about Moses, Elijah, Abraham and all the others mentioned in Scripture, He is aware of every situation. Everything we see today is temporary and God wants to speak to us about eternity. All of us who accept Jesus into our hearts and lives are promised time spent with Him forever, and He illustrates this to us in His Word, so that although Noah faced the floods, he came out of it alive and was guaranteed peace with God. You can look at the stories that happened thousands of years ago and if they don't seem particularly relevant to you, you can trust they are relevant to somebody. That's what the Bible is all about, God speaking into our lives.

Try not to spend your time struggling to pronounce the names, God's into the meaning, not the sound, thank goodness! Darren has had the opportunity to meet with lots of people on his travels, to visit lots of exciting places and to experience things most of us only dream of. How does he manage to make time for his Bible reading?

It can be different each week for me working in this sporting environment but you have to learn not to beat yourself up about it. God knows your heart and He understands. You have to be careful not to let the enemy use it against you, telling you you're a bad Christian if you missed a day, just try and get back into it the next day or whenever you can. It's so important to come to His word regularly so you really should be setting time aside to do it, but not under pressure. Give it over to God, think of Jesus like a real person and talk to Him in prayer. I always speak to Him like I would one of my friends and if I do miss a day's reading, I'm not going to beat myself up about it, I'm going to try and read it the next day and make time for doing it.

So, having a thrilling football career and serving the Lord is no excuse for Darren neglecting his Bible, I guess watching him play is no excuse either! All this talk about the Bible being His Word, Jesus being the Lord of this book, how can we be sure, how does the Bible prove He is who he says he is?

Too many miracles happened in the Bible. You can either accept the Bible is the truth or not. In my life I believe it's the absolute truth, every word that's written in it, too much of what I've read has happened or touched me for it to be false. I believe it proves Jesus was crucified, died and rose again on the third day, fulfilling earlier Scripture and I believe He is still alive today.

Actually, four different accounts testify to His death and resurrection, perhaps there is something in it! Well, even if we believe it to be the truth, isn't it just a glorified rulebook, designed to stop us having *any* fun?

Where there are lists of things to avoid, it's for your own good. If God commands you not to steal, commit adultery or even murder, then it's because He loves you and knows it's for your own good. People think it's all doom and gloom when you become a Christian, but I have never been happier in my life. God sees the harm that certain things do to us and He wants to protect us, that's why for example, He wrote the Ten Commandments.

Doom and gloom are not words you would use to describe this six-feet-tall giant of a guy, he rarely has a smile off his face and he has an infectious laugh he uses a lot, with a heart to tell others of his joy in the Lord, not exactly miserable then, this Christianity! People often talk about the Bible being the living word of God, eh, what? Don't like to be over cynical about this, but living? As Darren opens and studies it, how exactly does it become the 'living' word of God?

Let's take something like the idea of God 'granting the desires of your heart', a promise found in God's word in **Psalm 37 v4**. People can apply this to asking for a Ferrari or something and it doesn't happen. God's word is not really living because He knows you don't need one. However, if we've read that in sickness we should go to our elders and let them lay on hands, and we do it, and are healed, that's God's word becoming 'living', that's it taking on flesh. God tells us to seek His kingdom first, when we start to do that and put Him and His ways first in our life then the words on the page of the Bible start to happen, start to become real to us, that's when His word is living, when we are reading, studying then applying it to our lives.

Living word, now that sounds good to me, especially when God talks in the Bible about meeting Him face-to-face, *awesome*!

We might be on a Bible study now, and setting aside time each day to read it, but what about those times when we want to hear from His word directly, where we want to open it up and find exactly the right words to comfort or encourage, to dry tears or give us strength to face something horrible? How do we turn to God through the Bible?

First and foremost you need to know your Bible from reading and studying. I'm a footballer and I know exactly what I'm doing in the game and how to play it. I've watched the game for many years, I've listened to my managers, read all the books, I know the laws and if I want to improve I know I've got to work harder in training. If I want to strike the ball better I know staying behind and practicing every day for ten days or so will greatly improve me. It's the same with reading the Bible, when you start meditating and spending time in His Word then when you need something in particular you can pull it out of your head. The only way to know exactly where to turn is to study His word. When you start reading His Word you also become more in tune with God and can hear His voice more quickly, so that helps you to understand.

Other Christians who are more experienced (and this doesn't always mean older) can be a great help to us, pointing us to particular places in the Bible. Does Darren remember someone guiding him to God's word? Or has anyone ever given him a particular passage?

Yes, all the time, once when I was at Bradford, my friend Wayne Jacobs gave me the Scripture 'the joy of the Lord is my strength'. I've also had fellow Christians who have come to me and said, whilst reading their Bible God gave them a particular verse or word for me. Sometimes I'll go to church and during the sermon it seems the pastor is speaking directly into my situation. You pick up words from music, tapes, sermons, friends, pastors, anywhere you come to hear God. It can be so powerful and it certainly happens a lot when you get deeper into a relationship with Him.

People can often be put off by someone coming to them saying that they have a 'word from God', especially if it's controversial. Be assured God does still speak to His children today and you should *always* check it with Scripture and with a pastor or other Christian friends. God's not in the business of spooking, He knows you and wants what's best for you! God's word is obviously powerful, the boxer Alex Arthur kept the words to **Matthew 12 v18** on his head guard and won Commonwealth Gold with it – go and look it up yourself! God certainly likes to speak to His children as often as possible and welcomes our turning to His word, but how does Darren read it? Is it just like a newspaper or is there a way to study it?

Sometimes when you meditate it's just looking at the passage, really studying His words to us. Let's look at the Lord's Prayer, you would take it line by line. Jesus begins by praying to His Father who is in Heaven which you'll find in **Matthew 6 vs9–13**, He is reminding us how high and above all things our Father is, how majestic God is and How powerful He is. That's only the first line but already those few of words have started us thinking. You begin to study the Bible when you do that with each word and phrase and it becomes like God opening up doors for us, we start to see things in the Bible we haven't seen before, we start our minds thinking about more than just the words that are written. Further in the Lord's Prayer, Jesus takes us through what we should be praying for in each day, asking God for exactly what we need. He teaches us that we should be asking not to be led into temptation but delivered from the evil one, the devil. Often we can just sit back, accepting the enemy is defeated and believing we don't need to fight him, but we do. The Bible tells us that the devil is roaming around like a lion. He knows how to tempt us, he is here to rob, steal and destroy and Jesus is teaching us that we need to ask God to protect us, after all, the devil knows your weaknesses and he will try anything to keep you from God's plans for you. The God that we serve is a God of love who gives us hope for the future, but the devil will come along and remind you of your past and try to make you doubt God's love or forgiveness. This is just in one line, one prayer, but that's how we meditate on His Word, take it line by line and ask God to reveal His meaning to us.

Powerful tool, this meditating on His Word, shouldn't be a chore but a pleasure, after all, it seems to contain so much at so many levels, move over JK Rowling, this book is *real*! Like anything we love and cherish the more time we spend with it the more we understand and recognise, hmmm. The power of God's word is often spoken about, many people seem to have the ability to quote heaps of Scripture at the drop of a hat (that really is a stupid saying!) so does Darren think it's important to be able to quote Scripture, and is there any point, other than sounding like a real nerd in a Sunday School quiz?

For me the easiest way to memorise is to write it down and then have it with me all day, when I'm brushing my teeth, in the car, anywhere, just keep memorising it. If you do that for a whole week you can really learn His Scripture well. I think it's important because it means when you are in any situation, good or bad, you can ask what would God say, how would He guide me? If you have all these verses and words in your head then you can turn to it at any time.

So memorising Scripture is not just a smart move for our own spiritual growth, it's a handy weapon against the works of the enemy, hmmm, more about him later. Okay, let's just say that the Bible is actually really great to read and we know that God can use it to talk to us here and now in the comfort of our own untidy rooms, wow! Does it matter if we're reading the new street Bible, or urban version, does God really get hung up on which version we use?

> I read the New King James version and it's reliable and certainly the Bible that God has used to speak to me most, to bring me closer to Him so I would recommend that one.

Darren has found the Bible that is in a language that speaks clearest to him – why not check out the different versions to find one that speaks clearly to you? We're sorted, we're reading our Bibles and really getting it, God is really quite chatty. How do we try and relate everything we are reading into our lives, erm, can we relate building an ark in the desert with taking our science exams?

> Of course, it's God's Word for us in everything. Take healing for example, we can only use and apply it today because we have read about it in the Bible, whether personally or someone's told us. God says throughout the Bible that He is the God who heals, that's why the Bible is relevant today. This is the way God reveals what He wants us to know and how to handle things such as sickness and fear. The Bible is our manual for life, we read it and know that whatever our situation tomorrow, God has been through it and He knows what we are about to face. It's His Word to let us know how much He loves us, cares for us, protects us, teaches us, heals us, it's His Word for life to you and I. God is all about love, He doesn't want us to be down and gloomy, He wants us to be happy and Christianity should be fun. God intends us to love Him, love others and love ourselves, imagine how good this world would be if we did that!

Just imagine! Then go and read your Bible. So, we've got it all together, we're reading our Bibles and shock, horror, it actually makes sense! God delights in you coming to His word, He wrote it just for you, every verse. Someone once said to treat it like a long letter from your loving, Heavenly Father and that's exactly what it is. It's a possession to treasure. For Darren, how does the Bible compare as a treasure to a Division 1 winner's medal?

Darren Moore will come and go in football with someone else waiting to step in. When I finish playing football and it's all over, God will still be there. His love is from everlasting to everlasting and He has planned every day of my life, there isn't a hair on my head that falls out that He doesn't know about. Football is great but it's nothing compared to this great love God has for you and I, that's what my faith is all about and that's why I read my Bible.

That's a valuable book! So, curl up on the couch or wherever, read it with friends or alone, just read it. Darren Moore is not some deranged loony with a bad perm, odd socks and a multicoloured tank top, he's a guy totally switched on to the fact that everything in life that is good comes from his Father in heaven, who loves him unconditionally and wants the very best for him, even sending His Son to die for Him. Darren can't get enough of hearing and speaking to this Heavenly Father and reading his Bible is his door to do that, the way to the truth that is Jesus, the author and perfector of our faith. Letters from your Father in heaven are read by your eyes, but reach your heart and change your life, now that's power! Open the book and find out what He is saying to you today.

Further Scripture reading

Mark 1 vs1–3

The beginning of the gospel about Jesus Christ, the Son of God. It is written in Isaiah the prophet: "I will send my messenger ahead of you, who will prepare your way" – "a voice of one calling in the desert, 'Prepare the way for the Lord, make straight paths for Him.'"

Psalm 1 v2–3

But his delight is in the law of the Lord, and on His law he meditates day and night. He is like a tree planted by streams of water, which yields its fruit in season and whose leaf does not wither. Whatever he does prospers.

Psalm 112 v1

Praise the Lord. Blessed is the man who fears the Lord, who finds great delight in His commands.

Colossians 1 v6

All over the world this gospel is bearing fruit and growing, just as it has been doing among you since the day you heard it and understood God's grace in all its truth.

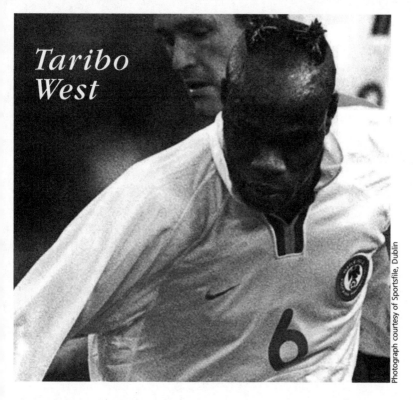

Taribo West

Photograph courtesy of Sportsfile, Dublin

DATE OF BIRTH: 26.03.74

POSITION: Central defender

CLUB HISTORY: Ibunkunoluwa FC, Sharks, Port Harcourt, Rangers International FC, Auxerre, Inter Milan, AC Milan, Derby County, Kaiserslautern, Partisan Belgrade, Plymouth Argyle

INTERNATIONAL HISTORY: Full caps for Nigeria

BEST EVER FOOTBALL MOMENT: Winning the UEFA Cup with Inter Milan in 1997, also Nigeria's performance at the 1996 Olympics where we won gold.

BEST EVER SPIRITUAL MOMENT: My conversion, which was so powerful. What happened to me as I received His Salvation was just an amazing experience, I felt God open up the gates in my life and release me into the destiny He has for me. I have seen miracles since and really awesome things done by Him, but nothing can compare with that moment when He first entered my life and filled me with His Spirit.

FAVOURITE ALL-TIME FOOTBALL ELEVEN: I have worked with, and watched, so many footballers that I love and respect, I couldn't pick just 11.

Taribo West
Going to church

Church, yawn, church, eh, do we have to? Church can seem like such a chore, after all, over one hour in one place is quite an alien concept to some, but is it important, do we really need to go? One person who clearly thinks so is former Inter *and* AC Milan, Auxerre, Derby County player and Nigerian international, Taribo West. He liked church so much, he started his own! Why?

> Church is the centre, a place where God can transfer His message to His people. The Bible says you shall know the truth and the truth shall set you free and I believe church is one of the places that God can bring revelation to you through His priest or minister. I started my church in Milan because I have seen how God has used my life to train and prepare me. There are things much bigger than football or luxury and I know God wants to use me to teach that message, so I felt in my spirit I should build a centre where people could come and hear the truth and be set free.

So, far from being a place of restrictions, Taribo believes church should set you free, wow!

Taribo has an extremely colourful life story (not too mention extremely colourful hair!) being born and raised in Port Harcourt, Nigeria, before being kicked out of his home by the time he was nine and moving to the streets of Lagos. Part of his youth and teens were spent running with the notorious gangs, getting involved in stealing, mugging, fighting and more, scraping around just struggling to exist in a very dark and often violent world. Taribo is the first to admit church and God were not very often on his mind.

> I came from a place where I had nothing, I was kicked out by my father when I was nine, then I lived on the streets struggling to survive. I didn't turn to God, I didn't realise who He was, I just kept doing what I needed to survive. It was a very difficult place to be, but at the time you don't know that, you just get on with it and find your own ways to make it through the day.

> What my background has taught me is that you need to try hard just to get by and you can never give up. What I now know, but didn't then, is that you cannot go a week without hearing the Word of the Lord, that is what has transformed me. It changed me from the inside out to make me the person I am today.

Whew, Taribo certainly tested God's forgiveness and love, yet look at him now! Does it mean that you have to get yourself sorted *before* you come to church? After all, if we are stuck in a dark place of sin or struggling with different problems, addictions, bad habits, won't God want us to stay away from His house?

> Church is an open arena, like a clinic. Whatever you are going through, physical or spiritual, you can come into church and be healed. I think the church is somewhere God has rendered open for everyone. God can refuel you and help you to become who He wants you to be. God accepts you however you are, on drugs, on crutches, with problems or without, His church is the centre for divine prosperity.

Well, what are we waiting for, we want some of that! So, after we decide to follow Jesus and to give Him our hearts, can't we just leave it at that, can't we have a relationship in the comfort of our own homes? Why do we need to gather with other people, after all, isn't our faith just between God and us?

> The Bible tells us to love your neighbour as we love ourselves,

the church community is a collective relationship, what I can't get in me I can get in you. God has given us all different talents and when we come together we can share them. God is love and when there is love it overcomes all things. That is why meeting with other Christians is important, we can all encourage one another to live for God's glory.'

The Christian faith is the truth and we need to be part of the bigger picture for Jesus, the body of Christ, His church, His people, aha, now I see why God is keen for us to attend! Church is not all about switching off as some preacher drones on for eternity about issues which seem irrelevant, church is the Lord's house, a place we can meet with Him, wow! So how do we find the right church for us, how do we know if we are presbyterian, pentecostal, evangelical, apostolic, brethren or something else altogether, do we choose a church or does church choose us?

I believe that in everything you should seek and ask His will in prayer, when you seek Him He will direct you to the church He has prepared for you. God has plans for all of us, for each day and that includes where we worship. God will bring us to the place where He can give us exactly what we need. You have to ask Him to lead you to the right church.

For some, church can be just the building; you know, all stained glass windows and pointy roofs, and meetings on a Sunday. Taribo's own church is a lively place with lots going on, a centre in Milan where people new to the city without friends or homes can come and hear the Word of the Lord.

One of the gifts God has blessed us with is praise. When you praise, the Bible says you will render the heavens open and that is one of the pursuits of our church, excellent praise. Our centre is also a place where you can come and be totally open and honest before God, a place where you can be saved and make a new start. God wants to give us the very best and our church is a place you can come and meet with him, whatever your circumstances.

Lively praise and getting saved, hardly sounds dull to me! Does it matter to God what the building is like and does He only come to a group of people in pews one day a week and go about fixing the world the other six days?

> I think the devil has been keeping people away from our churches with lies. Church is about coming into a relationship with our Father, getting closer to God. It is not about the building or getting into a relationship with a minister, we need to know Christ and let Him into our hearts, that's where church is. We pray that God will break down these barriers that have been put up. When the Word of God enters your heart, then you have the power, you can be influential for Him any day of the week!

Excellent, church is where God is when His people, even just two, are gathered to praise and to seek Him in worship, simple. Not to mention getting a blast of Heavenly power from hearing His Word. So what difference can the right church make in your life?

> One of the reasons you need to be planted in a church is you need to be hearing His Word. When you have had a rebirth experience your soul is saved and transformed, but you have to work on your mind and body too. Any time the mind or body is far from the soul you need a bridge and that can be the church. If you are in the right church and being transformed you can be more effective in your family or community. It's okay to worship from home at times too, but it's so important to seek the church God has for you and to keep moving in the direction He wants you to go. When people begin to see Christ in you and the changes in your life from going to church and knowing God, then they are challenged too and can be encouraged to come to Him.

Quite powerful then this church going! So we have found the right church, we like the music, the sermons and the folk. Now, does Taribo really believe it's bad for us to miss it, surely it's just good that we go, not harmful if we miss it?

From my experience, if I miss church for a while then I have no life in me. It's like a seed that a farmer has planted, you have to protect it, nurture it. I need to hear the Word of God every week to survive Monday to Monday, after everything God has done for me, when that church bell rings I need to be there, first in line. My faith is more important than anything in this world.

Okay, church – a place we should be rejoicing in as often as possible. What if it's not always possible to make it every week? For Taribo football has taken him all over the world, so how does he handle it when he just can't make church, when he has to miss it?

I have a lot of tapes and books that I read, plus the Lord has connected me with a lot of men of God who I speak with. When I was in England clubs started making a big deal about my insistence on being at church and being a pastor, it eventually stopped some signing me. I decided when I went to Partisan Belgrade I should be a true disciple at my work, sticking to their training regime. I must be disciplined in football, especially as some people are looking up to me. It is difficult if I can't make church but I never let a week go past without hearing and seeking the Word of God.

So, no excuses, coming to worship and meeting with other Christians is an important part of our faith journey, singing and dancing to God are scriptural, looks like we need to get to church then, and if we really can't make it, looks like church has to come to you via books, CDs and DVDs, anything that allows you to hear His Word and come closer to Him! The Bible tells us that church is the collection of believers, Christ's people. We're in church when we go to meet with them but we also *are* church in this world. Don't let this confuse you – we all need to find the right fellowship and teaching to fuel our fire and passion for God, we also need to *be* on fire and passionate. *Go* to church to receive and start *being* church to others!

Footballers are paid very well when they are at the top of their sport and can afford to dig deep for the offering plate, that's fair enough. However, what about the rest of us? One thing we often hear about in church, is 'tithing', basically giving a portion of your income to God in thanksgiving. Eh, does that mean pocket money or weekend jobs wages? How much should we tithe and what is it for?

> Give and it shall be given unto you, says the Bible. However, people are deceived about tithing, or giving to God and are more dependent on money than they are on God. God wants us to live in abundance. He will give you more. The Bible tells us that God will pour out blessings on us, our cups will run over, but we have to trust Him and give in faith. When you don't have much, you give what you do have to God and you'll discover He will give to you. In the Old Testament God's people were encouraged to give a tithe, a tenth, of what they had. Worship then is about what we can give to God, not what He can give to us, but you should wait and expect.

So, in giving we are getting blessed, that makes it so much easier. God has promised to provide everything you ever need, not necessarily everything you ever want. Ferrari's seem to take a long time arriving, but He promises He will provide so much more than we could ever dream of, if we just trust Him and accept His love and His guidance. He is good and we should always be grateful for how much He has given us already. Anyone who has very little by means of money should give of that little and pray a lot! Taribo has been blessed by an abundance of talent on the football pitch and he has certainly used it. Often the man of the match and certainly never less than 100 per cent committed in every tackle and run. God has certainly given him this talent, yet can he use it for the good of his church? Can we who have no obvious talents like being musical or able to preach or act still turn our talents into something which benefits our church?

> All my life everything I have done God has given me. I believe God wants to use me as a channel to help other people, to share this truth and love for God with them. All my earnings and talents I give to God, I use it for the ministry and that is the

best kind of love, to give Him everything, the best I can do for God. God gave us all talents, the best thing we can do is to use them for His Kingdom, whatever they are.

No excuses then, if you are a talented knitter, get knitting for God, footballer, dancer, shelf-stacker, whatever, just do it well and do it for Him! While we are becoming the creatures God intended us to be, praying, Bible reading, attending church and polishing our shiny halos, He has His work cut out with others! The one thing which can often spoil a church is *the congregation*! How do we cope with the fact that we are thrown together with a bunch of folks who, at times, seem a million miles away from us on the human-being scale? Why do other Christians sometimes seem determined to disagree or cause problems? How does Taribo cope with the fact that our fellow worshippers can often be the most testing of companions?

> Pray for God to give you the grace to forgive. When you forgive people who annoy or offend you, God gives you favour. The Bible tells us to bless those who persecute you, pray for our enemies and any time you do that God will lift you to another level. I think if God brings people who annoy you around you, there must be a reason for it and I just keep praying He equips me to deal with it.

So, we have to actually practise this 'love your neighbour thing', hhmmm. Church can be a place of giving as we have discussed, tithing is scriptural but it is also a place of receiving, huh? Church is a sanctuary, a safe place, where we can meet with God through His Word and worship, a place where God can come and meet with us. So has Taribo ever had that, a sense that God has designed a service especially for him, with a message or word?

> It happens all the time, through song, through His Word, even through young people. Part of my ministry is to disciple young people, to train them for leadership and it can be really powerful the way God uses them to teach me or to speak to me. It can be a wonderful encouragement, a revival to put you back on track. It often happens to me in worship that God speaks to me.

Wow, that's enough to send me running *into* church, instead of the other way round. I want my Heavenly Father to talk to me, and I want Him to teach me through His Word, awesome. Church then, needn't be a chore, but rather a Holy Place, a place in our week where we can put our worries and troubles aside and just worship our Creator. We might be having a tough time, we might be having a ball, but we should always make time for Him, to give thanks and to pray for His continued guidance and love. Taribo has certainly got a lot going for him and yet he is the first to admit that it counts for nothing without Jesus. Taking time to go to His house once a week is nothing!

> What I love about church is it's the cheapest entertainment in the world! Discos, theatre, cinema all take money, but at church you have good messages, God will bless you with His Word, you have an entertainment ministry and the presence of God will be there with His anointing. All these things you can't get from the world. This is the exclusive glory which I love in the gathering of the church.

Enthusiasm aplenty! A big influence in our Church and worship is the person at the front, the pastor, preacher, minister, priest, vicar, brother, sister, whatever you want to call the guy or girl who heads it. So, how important is our church leader, how much authority should they have?

> I often describe the pastor as the highest in the Church. He is the one with authority in the Church and the strength of the pastor is often the strength of the Church. We really need to pray hard for God to guide us to the right church and pastor so we can understand the pastor's vision then support it. Not every Church is meant to be a mega church, small ones can be very effective in their communities, you just need to keep checking you are being true to the task God has given you as a church. The Bible always speaks about the hand of God being on His people and you should be able to see that in your Pastor. We need to work under people to hear from God and it's so important to respect your Pastor.

Taribo is able to speak about this as he pastors a Church himself, so, does that mean he is perfect, never sinning or giving into temptation, never straying from the right path?

> No, not at all. There are a lot of responsibilities as a Pastor and the further you go in your walk there are more temptations and problems. I believe it's all about trust and the Lord. In my own ministry I work with people who have real problems, people limping through life and I want to get alongside and help any way I can. Pastors are still human and they can make mistakes but it's with the power of Jesus that we can do the work God has set for us. If we work in this dimension, in the power of Christ, then I think we can overcome whatever problems come along. That is what my ministry is, accepting people who are limping and with human weaknesses just like me, and working together with God to see His Kingdom advance.

So, your church leaders are human and dependent upon God – I suppose Jesus is a stunning example of what a church leader should be like. During his time with his disciples he not only taught them, he served them – on one occasion, which we can read about in the Bible, in **John 13 vs1–17**, we see him washing his disciples' feet – yuk, a task usually reserved in those days for the servant in the house! Perhaps you should wait awhile before taking off your trainers and shoving your smelly feet in his or her face – but you get my drift, our church leaders are human, they will make mistakes and get it wrong, but, they should truly have a heart to try to be like Jesus in all they think, say and do (don't be smug, so should we!). At all times you should be able to check your Pastor's advice/ message/sermon/requests with Scripture and see that it is in keeping with God's Word. If you are having doubts or concerns about your pastor, speak to other people in your Church or other Christians.

Taribo is honest enough to say he is tempted or faces problems like us all, your Pastor isn't perfect, but God's Word is. Some of us have a mad notion that God is concerned with our trainers or our hairstyles or our jeans, tops, make-up, jewellery or piercings –

wrong! He cares about our hearts, minds, souls, words, thoughts and actions, so does it matter how we are dressed?

> God is not concerned about your colour, your hair, what clothes you wear, He is concerned with your heart. God will guide and direct you and He will make changes on the inside, just come as you are.

There we have it, get off your backsides and go. God doesn't care what you wear or how you look, He cares about what's happening on the inside, after all He created you. Don't let your church life suffer because you don't like the first one you try, *persevere*. God has asked us to come together to sing songs and to pray and read Scripture, not to test us but to help us stay on the right path, to help us come to Him and give Him the glory. Football can be like a church for some, coming together to worship at the feet of 22 false idols at times! How does Taribo cope with all the adoration and praise, after all, it should be going to God and yet people don't seem to want to know the creator of Beckham and Co, preferring the creation!

> I believe God is building a people of influence in the world of football. You can minister at many levels and I thank God that He is using me to minister in this arena. You can try and be a light in the world you are in and make a difference, whatever that is. I am very careful of the temptation that comes with the blessings of success, adoration and fame. It is very important to recognise that something which can build you up can also bring you down. I have tried to draw a line where I know that if glory comes, it is honour to Him and I give it back to Him.

Whew, keep on turning to God with the bad things and the good, after all if things are going badly, turn to Him for strength and comfort, if things are going well, turn to Him with thanksgiving, He is in control of everything. I love this fact: God, who made *all* things, made me and is in control of my life if I let Him! Awesome! Taribo has scaled the heights in an impressive club and international career and he has been an ambassador for the Lord on his travels, how do we do likewise? For all of us, an international football career isn't an option (shame!), but we still have a role to play, how do we be church in our world?

> We should be a light to the world. When we are Christians we need to abide in the Word of the Lord and when people know you are one, then they want to see how you act, how you are different. My prayer is that all Christians will be touched by the fire of the Holy Spirit and that they will go out and touch others, bringing them to His Kingdom.

So, what kind of church is not really a question about buildings or songs, it's a question about hearts and spirit. Taribo West has graced the pitches of some of the world's greatest stadiums, played alongside and against some of the world's finest players. However, it's his passion for serving God and fulfilling his calling of ministering to others which drives him on. Taribo has a job which can open doors but it's his all-consuming faith in Jesus which he uses to open eyes and ears, trusting God to open hearts as he preaches and ministers in his church. When the boots are finally hung up on this Super Eagle's career, you know that Taribo will move into full time ministry, after all, this guy doesn't just go to church, He has one. Do you?

Further Scripture reading

1 John 1 v3
We proclaim to you what we have seen and heard, so that you also may have fellowship with us. And our fellowship is with the Father and with His Son, Jesus Christ.

Psalm 113 vs1–2
Praise the Lord. Praise, O servants of the Lord, praise the name of the Lord. Let the name of the Lord be praised both now and for evermore.

Acts 2 v46–47
Every day they continued to meet together in the temple courts. They broke bread in their homes and ate together with glad and sincere hearts, praising God and enjoying the favour of all the people. And the Lord added to their number daily those who were being saved.

Revelation 2 v17
He who has an ear, let him hear what the Spirit says to the churches. To him who overcomes, I will give some of the hidden manna. I will also give him a white stone with a new name written on it, known only to him who receives.

Dirk Heinen

DATE OF BIRTH: 03.12.70

POSITION: Goalkeeper

CLUB HISTORY: Bayer Leverkusen, Denizlispor, Stuttgart, Eintracht Frankfurt

INTERNATIONAL HISTORY: Under-18 and Under-21 caps for Germany

BEST EVER FOOTBALL MOMENT: Every moment I play and win.

BEST EVER SPIRITUAL MOMENT: The birth of my children (God's greatest gift).

FAVOURITE ALL-TIME FOOTBALL ELEVEN (*4/4/2 formation*):

		Schumacher		
Förster	Beckenbauer		Netzer	Jorginho
Zidane	Keane		Giggs	Pele
	Henry		G Müller	

FAVOURITE PIECE OF SCRIPTURE: All of the Bible.

Dirk Heinen

How to cope when things go wrong

L ife, as we have discovered by now, isn't always a bed of roses (which would be pretty uncomfortable anyway!) and even though we're in a relationship with our Heavenly Father, bad stuff happens.

One footballer who is all too aware of this is Dirk Heinen, goalkeeper with VFB Stuttgart in the German Bundesliga. He's enjoyed many highs and lows both on and off the pitch and admits to his share of heartache and trauma, yet he is strong and certain in his love of the Lord. Football is his pleasure but Jesus is his passion. This guy loves the Lord and wants the world to know it! Dirk has been a Christian since he was 23 and is very honest about his faith.

> When my sister died of cancer in 1994, it really opened my eyes. She was only 38 and it was a terrible time, really hard for me. Before she died I thought I had everything and all I thought about was football. I had been playing football professionally for four years and thought I had it all; girls, money and cars, everything, but it really meant nothing at all. That was in August, and in December of that year I met my wife Sandra, from Ireland. She began to talk to me about Jesus, telling me stories from the Bible. I began to read the Bible for myself and to really look at my life. I realised it wasn't that

good and I turned to God and told Him if He was real, He should take my life and make the best out of it. He did. That was in December 1994 and He has been with me ever since I gave my life to Him.

So Dirk changed his ways and asked God into his life, realising something was missing, recognising it was God. Isn't that the end of any problems, shouldn't life be stress-free from that moment on? Surely becoming a Christian ought to guarantee life's a breeze?

I think everything is a little bit easier because our Heavenly Father has our lives in His hand, but it doesn't mean there are no problems. Being a Christian means that God knows everything that happens to me and He has everything in His hand. When something bad does come into my life or my family's life, I give it over to Him, I trust Him with it. I know He wants the best for me and brings me through it.

So, although you still have to suffer sometimes as a Christian, God is with you and steers you through. Hmmm, becoming a Christian for many people is a very difficult step, for others it's a natural response to a Christian upbringing. However you come to know God, you can be sure He is in every step you take to reach Him. One thing that's very important to a footballer is fitness and for a goalkeeper psychological fitness is especially important, a healthy mind is a must between the posts! A real test of Dirk's faith came when, despite a good prayer life, he suffered a severe head injury which took him out of the game for months, *ouch*!

A week before the start of the season, during a friendly, I tried to save a free kick and was hit by either a foot or a knee on my skull, just above my eye. It was completely smashed, I had to get a metal plate inserted and they said I was fortunate it hadn't been just a little higher as I might have had brain damage. Even as I was being stretchered out, I was singing worship songs and saying, 'God, everything is in your hands'. I was scared, really scared but I also knew that Jesus was in control and I had a sense of peace. I knew that God would make everything okay, no matter how bad the injury was. For the first three months I couldn't train and then for the next 18 months I was on the bench as the team had signed a new goalkeeper and he turned out to be good. It was so hard for me, such a long time to be a substitute, especially in this game.

Ah, imagine watching your replacement play as you sit on the bench! So how do we cope when we've been praying, often for a specific thing to happen or not, and the very opposite occurs. How do we cope when it goes pear-shaped? Wasn't Dirk angry that God allowed him to be injured?

Even now when I look back I can see that God used it for good. When I was injured, we'd just had our first son and I was able to spend so much time with him, it was so special. At this level in football you have to travel within Europe, go to away games and we spend so much time away from home. You can't get these first years back with your kids and I think God knew how important it was that I should be able to be there for him and my wife.

Does that mean that it is pointless to pray, worship or read Scripture, after all, we are not in control of other people's actions, far less God's will?

I think we should pray then leave the result to Jesus, to our Father in heaven. We should have some targets in our lives, some vision, but after praying about them we should trust God. I want to work for Jesus and after 18 months of being on the bench at Bayer Leverkusen, I was offered a move to Frankfurt. I prayed about it and asked God, telling Him I would move if it was His will and that I wanted to be a light for Him at Frankfurt, that's exactly what happened. A couple of players used to come to my home and have a Bible study and they came back to the Lord, so that was definitely an answer to prayer. He has everything in His hand and He knows what is good for us. Even now at Stuttgart He is answering my prayers, we have three Christians in the team and very good fellowship, so I know that prayers are powerful and very important.

Aha, praying actually works then, when we let God be God! So, continuing along our walk, praying, praising, seeking is not only important when things are working, it's vital when they are not. Dirk also has the support of his wife and family and, of course, the lads in the dressing room. For most of us friends are important but not always there 24/7. We can also try to be too independent, thinking we are being a pain if we talk about our troubles, preferring to talk to the pillow instead. Often though a fresh perspective or a wise word from another is a big help. How important is it to turn to others when we are in a mess, when we really can't see a way out of the darkness?

> It's really important to have fellowship, people you can turn to. I can't always get to church because we have to train on Sundays, so to have my team mates who will join me in Bible study is wonderful. Last year I was in Turkey and it was very difficult for us, but people like Dietmar Ness from *Athletes In Action* came to visit and pray with us, that meant so much and really empowered me. Christian friends can really be a help during the dark times, so I think we should all try to find others we can share our life with, good and bad.

What strikes me as being unfair as a Christian is when you are really trying to 'walk the walk', but life seems a big uphill struggle. Meanwhile folks you know, who have no interest in God or, in fact, in their fellow human beings seem to sail through life without a worry – maddening! Isn't God watching, doesn't Dirk get mad that others are having it easy?

> It seems like that, but it's not often the case. Look at footballers, they seem to have everything, but deep inside there may be something missing. I used to look forward to winning a championship, getting promotion, a bigger car maybe, but when you achieve it you think, "what next?" What do you really have – *nothing*. People may seem to be having it all but often they are empty on the inside, never satisfied or fulfilled. It's so

different when you take Jesus into your heart though, then you have His peace and His power, you don't need anything else.

Dirk has recently left Turkey, a Muslim country; so how difficult was it to be in a place so openly opposed to his Christian beliefs?

Once again we prayed really hard that if we went to Turkey we could be used by God, we could be lights for Him. It was very difficult, after all you could have been killed just for being a Christian. Again God used us and I used to have some great discussions with my team mates, they would also come to my room to study the Bible and to discuss our faith. God certainly had His hand in this time, bringing us into contact with people from Finland and the Czech Republic as well as the guys from Turkey. We had people from all over and we often shared our faith. My wife would try to minister to the other wives while the players were away, telling them stories and praying. It was hard for my family, especially my eldest son who was very much the outsider at kindergarten.

I suppose when you think that a little hassle or even a really traumatic time on earth may be rough, then we do have an eternity in the presence of true love, joy, peace and happiness to look forward to!

Dirk has faced tough times as a Christian and come out the other side. Sometimes it's not always a 'biggy' which holds us back or steals our smiles, it's often a constant little thing, you know, like failing at something or being the butt of jokes, how do we cope when it's little things that go wrong? Can we go to God just for a grumble?

God has everything in His hands, big or small, so, of course we should talk to Him about everything. We're told to come to Him like little children and I've really learned what this means after praying with my own kids. They want to thank God for things like the sunshine, a nice play and I've learned to thank God for these things too. If you're going through a hard time, even if it seems trivial, tell Him about it, after all He loves you and wants what is best for you. He cares. He's there for us in everything and there is nothing that is too big or too small.

God has promised to be there for us, every minute, every step of the way, even in the darkest places – awesome! Often we feel pain for others, it's when our mates or relatives are struggling that we can hurt too. How does Dirk cope when it goes pear-shaped for people he loves?

> This can be such a difficult time when it's other people hurting, but we still have to take it to God, turn to Him for guidance and support. There was a situation in Frankfurt when a team mate's niece died. He came to me and asked me all sorts of questions, "Was she in heaven or hell? Why did she die?" I'd had no relationship with this guy before and I really didn't know what to say. I asked Jesus what He wanted me to do as I found this all very difficult. I just wanted to make it better for him. Sometimes it's better to say nothing, just listen and be there. I spoke to another Christian about it, asked for their help, and they told me I should keep listening to him, set aside time for this guy. I really had to grow in this time, but I believe it's been important to pray for him and just to be there, to give him someone to talk to.

For those of us who have prayed for others and seen results, it's indeed a blessing, and often the way God chooses to bring His children back to Him, restore them to their faith. Perhaps we should be more thankful when things are going well, after all, God is in the good times for sure. Has going through a time of trial made Dirk more appreciative of the good things God has done for him?

> Sure! If there's a bad thing, I see it as right for me at that time. If I'm walking on the right path then the Devil will come along and try to knock me off target, stop me achieving. However, good times or bad, if we give it all to God then He will bring out the best for us. The bad times can help us to grow and to change as well.

Praise the Lord! When we look around we really do have a lot to give thanks for! Dirk may be seen to be in a privileged position, playing for a team he loves, in a sport he loves, but as we have read it's not always straightforward. He's been able to come out the other side though. Does he think the experience has been useful to him?

> Absolutely, there have been so many opportunities to tell others and to serve God. When I gave my life to Him in 1994 I was so happy. I wanted to tell everyone every time I was interviewed about my football, every newspaper, camera or radio; I talked about Jesus even when some of the reporters just turned away. My injury even offered me the chance to share my faith, to let people know what Jesus did for me. So even the times of trouble can be used for good by God and He has certainly given me opportunities in the dark times.

So, not only can we be assured we will come out the other side of our troubles when we trust in God, we can actually use it to help others, now that's good! Perhaps we need to be more open in letting God in on all our worries, after all, He did make the earth in six days, and perhaps He can work out how to get our lives back on track or how to help our friends, hmmm. Trouble can often be the result of our own making. Yes, uncomfortable though it may make us (especially if it means our parents can say I told you so!) we often find ourselves in a mess because of things we've done or haven't done. We know that there are certain things God wants us to avoid and certain things He wants us to embrace, sometimes we do the opposite. Is it really fair to turn to Him when it's our fault and will He listen?

> Of course we should turn to God whenever there is a problem, no matter whose fault it is. If my children do something wrong, get into a mess and then come to me and say they need help, of course I will help them. I'm their father and I love them, it's exactly the same with God. If we turn to Jesus, He will help us. It's easy for me to turn to Him, that's why He died on the cross.

If we turn from God's ways and go our own only to discover we get in a big, horrible, scary mess with lots of problems – don't make it worse by staying away from Him, turn back and ask for His help. He truly loves you and will sort it out for your good! A word which can seem heavy and condemning is *repent*, yet what it really means is admitting you are sinning, or making a mess, telling God you are sorry then asking for His forgiveness – simple. His forgiveness doesn't take long to arrive either as He promises in the Bible that it shall be given immediately. He has already sent Jesus to pay the price; He was waiting on you turning to Him, *awesome*! Dirk may, or may not, face more troubles in his life yet at all times he turns to Christ for guidance. It seems that the more he trusts in the Lord, the less he gets hassled by what life throws at him.

> Absolutely, because God accepts us as His children then He takes the load off our shoulders. In everything I find that God has our best interests at heart so we have to give Him our problems and trust Him to sort them, in His way.

Dirk has truly discovered God's peace in his life and therefore faces all life's hassles with a kind of spiritual shield, now that sounds impressive! Of course, being the good little Christians we are we know persecution for Christ's sake is in fact a blessing, as we will be rewarded in Heaven, eh? What does that actually mean and how do we know we are being persecuted for our faith? Does that include people taking the mickey because we are believers?

> I have never personally experienced anybody laughing at me, at least not face-to-face, because of my beliefs but I know it happens. Also, today there is still persecution of Christians all over the world in places such as Jerusalem, Ireland and China. However people must persevere and know that God is with them.

If we are ever persecuted for our faith, laughed at, jeered or ignored, hold tight to the promise that God is with you and will reward you in heaven if you stay true to Him. Also pray for those whose lives are in danger, who risk beatings and death simply for having a Bible or saying a prayer – puts getting called a geek once in a lifetime into perspective! So our journey with and to the Lord is not always straight and plain-sailing but it is certainly true and leading us to glory. Dirk has reached a place of trust and commitment in his walk with God, he has surrendered his life to God's will and has discovered the blessing of true fellowship with others and God. He's finding God's will daily, wow! So what now for Mr Heinen, how will he stay this close to God, leaning on Him through thick and thin?

> Through prayer, worship, the Bible and also through love. God has given me great love through my beautiful wife, Sandra, and my wonderful kids, Cormac and Kylie. God will always send someone along our path to strengthen and keep us in touch with our faith, all you have to do is recognise the people and the signs!

For this keeper of the faith those signs of love, joy and peace far outweigh the bad times, the times Dirk also sees as spiritual growth and part of his journey. Times will come where we are forced to suffer, either physically or mentally, yet hold tight to the promises we read in His word. Our God has only good things planned for us – Jesus Christ has shed His blood to see us through the difficult times, just keep trusting in Him. Life may seem hectic, scary and imbalanced right now, but better times are coming and you have a Saviour who will hold you till they arrive!

Further Scripture reading

Romans 5 v3

Not only so, but we also rejoice in our sufferings, because we know that suffering produces perseverance; perseverance, character; and character, hope.

Psalm 119 v50

My comfort in my suffering is this: Your promise preserves my life.

Psalm 125 v2

As the mountains surround Jerusalem, so the Lord surrounds His people both now and for evermore.

James 5 vs13–14

Is any one of you in trouble? He should pray. Is anyone happy? Let him sing songs of praise. Is any one of you sick? He should call the elders of the church to pray over him and anoint him with oil in the name of the Lord.

Richard Rufus

DATE OF BIRTH: 21.01.75

POSITION: Central defender

CLUB HISTORY: Charlton Athletic
Play-off Division 1 winners in 1998 (promoted into the Premiership)
Won the Division 1 league in 2001 (promoted into the Premiership)

INTERNATIONAL HISTORY: Under-21 caps for England

BEST EVER FOOTBALL MOMENT: 1) Scoring my first goal at Wembley 2) Playing in the Premiership 3) Playing for England under-21 team.

BEST EVER SPIRITUAL MOMENT: It would have to be when I gave my life to the Lord and became a born-again Christian, also when I was baptised, because from that moment on my Christian life with God started. And from that point my life has been filled with so much joy, peace, and the blessings of the Lord. At times though I still have my fair share of trials as most Christians do. But the joy of the Lord, which is my strength, overcomes all these things. For example, when I think about becoming a

Christian, I feel really blessed and privileged because the Bible says in **Romans 8 v29** that *For those God foreknew he also predestined to be conformed to the likeness of his Son ....* In other words before the world was created God called and chose me to become a Christian (His adopted son) and all this happened before I was even born! See **Jeremiah 1 v5** – that's why this is one of best spiritual moments in my life.

FAVOURITE ALL-TIME FOOTBALL ELEVEN (*4/4/2 formation*):
As you can see the team I've picked is an all-star international team with players from many countries.

	Buffon		
Cafu	Baresi	Adams	Maldini
Beckham	Dunga	Zidane	Cruyff
	Pele	Ronaldo	

FAVOURITE PIECE OF SCRIPTURE: Where do I start? There are so many verses to choose from. However, having thought about it, I would say the most meaningful Scripture would have to be **Luke 9 v25** because this Scripture was a turning point in my life just before I became a Christian. When I analysed my life without Christ and put things into perspective I realised how this verse of Scripture is so true, but not only to my life, but to the lives of many others as well.

Richard Rufus
How to handle being different

So, we are called to pray, read our Bible, go to church, just your average 'one of the crowd' lifestyles then, *not*!

Christianity is a life changing, inspirational, mind-blowing transformation; it also makes us different from everyone else. One person who has experienced life on both sides of the Jesus divide is former Charlton footballer, Richard Rufus. Richard was a professional footballer for 13 years until injury forced his retirement in 2004.

He has been a Christian for seven years and is well aware that life as a non-Christian has a lot less guidelines, in fact anything goes.

> Before I was a Christian I did what I wanted, when I wanted. I used to go clubbing all the time, get up late, then after training just hang around with my mates and went with the flow of whatever was happening. I was happy for a moment, but once I had been there and done it sort of thing, I still felt an emptiness inside that wouldn't go away. After I had achieved my dreams of playing football professionally and internationally (captaining England under-21's) before I was even 21, I realised that there had to be something more to life, even though I had everything I had always wanted. I had finally made it as a professional footballer yet I still wasn't content.

Life for Richard may have seemed simple and easy but equally it left him feeling empty inside. On becoming a Christian he discovered that as well as finding the 'missing peace' he also began to discover he was different from the way he was before and to his surprise different from those around him. Oops, what does that mean?

> God has chosen us to be His holy people, a people set apart for Himself. As a result, our attitudes, actions and our belief in Him are what set us apart. Though we are in the world, we must not be of it, that is, not letting certain things of this world change and influence our lives that are contrary to our faith in God; for example the spirit of idolatry, envy, hatred, etc, cannot live in our hearts. As believers, we mustn't think this gives us license to be totally separated and isolated; actually we should be positively influencing the dying world by the sharing of His gospel. We are called to be the salt of the earth and light to the world. Wherever we go we should try and carry this hope that is in us to others.

Phew, so we don't need to move into the church hall, we just need to let our relationship with Jesus keep us from following the wrong path. Set apart, hmm, isn't life strange, we seek the Lord, find Him, accept His great love and compassion, then get set apart, while we are then commissioned to love our neighbours – confused? How can we love our neighbours when we are set apart from them?

> Set apart doesn't mean we have to be alienated from other people who need our help. The parable Jesus mentioned about the Samaritan helping the man left half dead by his attackers is a prime example for us to follow. We must love our neighbour not only with words but also our deeds, though this can be hard when it means praying for those who persecute you. Such love though demonstrates we are children of God; after all, the Bible says even pagans and tax collectors greet only their friends. God extends His love to everyone, causing the sun to rise on the good and the evil and sends rain on the righteous and the unrighteous.

Aha, so to really love our neighbours, we also have to set them a loving example. Richard became a Christian, accepting Jesus as his saviour and he would never turn back to life without him, although he admits it's not always easy 'walking the walk', so how does he stay on the right track, following God at all times?

By having a daily commitment to prayer and Bible study – that is a key part of my life. I am blessed that our church has a time where we meet for an hour each week for fellowship, Bible study, praising and worshipping God and encouraging one another. I also travel quite a bit to share my faith with other groups and churches and that keeps me on track with my saviour.

Richard had to share his lifestyle and beliefs with his team mates, that can't always have been easy, after all, life as a footballer can lead to great temptations. How does he cope with seeming like a goody two shoes (it's an old saying, I know!)?

It's never really been an issue since I became a Christian for my life is governed by what the Bible says and not what other people's opinions are. I know whom I believe in and what He has done for me. His grace is sufficient. That's why it's so important to build up our relationship with God and really know Him for any hard times ahead. You have got to be strong and refuse to go with the flow, however that means there may be people who want to persecute you for what you believe. No servant is better than his master, and Jesus was persecuted, therefore we can expect similar treatment as we pick up our cross and follow Him.

You can tell while speaking to Richard his faith is unshakeable, so too is his inner strength. This guy is not just a servant for the Lord, he is a mighty warrior! Being a Christian brings unequalled blessings and peace, and as it leads to eternal life (**John 3 v16**) we know it's lasting. What can be fleeting however, is our resolve. We might intend to stay sober, never touch drugs, refrain from sex before marriage, never gossip about another, but try explaining that to our mates who don't have our faith, eh, do we have to? Doesn't that make us even more isolated?

I could never keep the gospel, the good news of Christ to myself! Whether it makes us isolated or not we have to be a faithful witness of the gospel in season or out of season. One of my prayers was for an opportunity to evangelise to my teammates so that they too can come to know Jesus. Some at the club might laugh and joke about my faith at times, but if they had a problem or a serious issue those same ones came to talk and even ask me to pray for them. I wouldn't have these opportunities if I didn't share my faith in the first place. It is so important to keep praying for those who haven't become Christians yet.

Not only should we never hide our faith from our mates, we should be praying that they too can come to know God. Richard had to retire early from the game he loves and has played all his life, so how does he cope with his time on the sidelines, after all, a footballer that doesn't play can't be happy. How does he stop from moaning, giving in to doubt and fear? Does he not have to be different during the difficult times too?

I try to get closer to God. It can be difficult when things aren't going your way, you can feel like the world is on your shoulders and wonder why all these things are happening when you are serving God, but I know the devil is a liar. In the Bible, in the book of Romans, it says all things work together for the good of those who love the Lord and from my own experience I know this to be true. It's also good to talk with your Christian friends, get uplifted. When I first came to the church, the very first time I had given my tithe, which is an offering to God's work, I came out to find my car broken into, the stereo stolen and tyres nicked. Also that year, during my debut in the Premiership I got sent off which was extremely harsh, then broke my wrist playing against Man Utd, and at the end of the season we were relegated. To top it all off I ruptured ligaments in my ankle in the last game of the season, leaving me on crutches for six weeks. All this and more in the first 18 months of being a Christian, but people told me just to hang in there. I did, and the next year God just turned everything around, we were champions of Division 1, we won promotion back up to the Premiership, I was offered a new contract, I scored six goals that season and missed only three games instead of the 15 I had missed the season before; it just gave me such hope – never give up.

So we can be effective witnesses by being consistently different, consistently thankful to our God and Maker even when we feel like joining the ranks of the mass moaners. Now that's a challenge! Life as a Christian can seem at times a bit complicated. We are learning more and more about God from His Word and His church, yet at the same time we're discovering how far we fall short of His standards. Sometimes it seems, no matter how hard we try, we still get it wrong. Should we just give up, go back to our worldly ways, after all, being different and getting it wrong anyway doesn't sound that clever to me?

> Certainly not! We have to realise that we are saved by grace and Jesus has paid the price for our sins. We cannot think we are unworthy and shouldn't give up even when we make mistakes. If we confess them, God forgives *all* our sins, He doesn't hold them against us.

So Richard believes we ought to keep on keepin' on, okay! Life as a young black footballer raised issues of racism, how did Richard cope with that?

> Unfortunately I just had to persevere with it. Football is trying hard to stamp it out and things are better, but unfortunately there is still some there. It could make you feel bad and before I was a Christian, bitter too, but now I just give it up to God.

I guess it's not just being a Christian that makes you different in this world; plenty of people want to hurt and alienate others for a whole variety of reasons (not got the right trainers, overweight, underweight, girlfriend/boyfriend problems etc). At least when we are Christians we have the love and protection of God to turn to, whew! Jesus managed to come to earth with a really unpopular, radical, revelationary message and still made masses of mates wherever he went, wow! So how do we manage to stay Christian and cool, followers and not freaks? How do we keep our faith and our friends?

> We can't compromise our faith for our friends. Sometimes it will be hard going, but if they are truly your friends they will understand and hopefully respect that. If we look into Jesus' life, He was radical and at times controversial, in the Bible in the book of Matthew, Chapter 10, we see this. I try and be a witness for Him, sowing seeds to my friends who don't believe with hope that God will do the rest. You may be the closest and last person they can have to knowing Christ, so take and make the most of every opportunity. It is strange for my mates to realise I am happier now than I was in the so called good old days!

Having a good bunch of friends around Him was really important to Jesus (even Judas for a time!) and we know He stuck to the job given to Him by His Father. I guess then we have no excuses for giving up! Richard is happy living in the London area. Even though he works in a city, he still goes home to a community, a community he belongs to or does he? Can we really be part of a group, gang or community, if we are intent on setting ourselves apart? Or can we only really belong to the church?

> I think we should be part of our community in the way we reach out into it. I truly believe one of the aims of the church is to send us out there to be what Jesus described as 'fishers of men'. Jesus told us to go and make disciples of all nations; we cannot keep our faith confined to our church building like some kind of elite Sunday morning club. The need is out there, and the harvest is ripe but the labourers are few, lets pray for more labourers.

So there we have it, we are called to be different from the world, we are expected to behave in a certain way, with love and compassion, but that doesn't mean we have to cut ourselves off from the world entirely, no, just cut ourselves off from that which harms us. Fitting in to the way of the world may not be what we want, and that's fine, but what if we don't fit in at all? How do we handle it if the fact that we don't want to be joining in the criticism or the cruel jokes, or the crude chat and language means we are isolated? What do we do when it seems our faith can make us Nigel-no-mates?

> It must be hard if you feel isolated and left out but just keep going. I must confess to compromising my beliefs a few times earlier in my faith just to join in, but I went home feeling so guilty it wasn't worth it. Persevere, and pray, keep seeking God for it will get better and He will reward your faith.

So, stick with Him, God will always be our mate, excellent! Richard has seen a huge change in his own life, his attitudes, his actions, all since he became a Christian. So what were the things God asked him to change? How did he become different?

> Through reading my Bible, I have changed and still am being changed, it's not an overnight thing. I think when I started to understand and discover more of His Word He used it to change me for my good. The Bible says we are saved from the moment we believe, but we have to work out our salvation. I think it is a process, we have to work on our attitude and our behaviour. When we read the Bible we should reflect on what we read, a doer not just a hearer of His Word!

At the end of the day, being a Christian is not all about struggle and sacrifice, we can smile as well. God wants us to reflect His ways in our lives, to shine for Him in all situations. Sometimes it seems we never get it right but we have to keep on trying. Yes it can be scary to be the lone voice saying '*No*' when your mates want to have some fly beers or quite frightening if you and your mates feel God wants you to share your faith with guys in your life who you think don't know Him. However, rest assured, He is always with you, in fact He has travelled ahead and prepared the way for you. Being different, Christian or not, can also be a lot of fun. Richard has been able to enjoy so much from his faith, it's not all about suffering, after all being different can mean being cool (just look at every Beckham haircut!). So what is it that makes Richard happy about being different for the Lord?

> There are so many things I could list. The main thing is the joy of the Lord. Money, cars, careers and all other material things will come and go but Jesus is with me forever. Just to think that God chose me to be saved even, as it says in Jeremiah, before I was in my mother's womb. Even when I was out partying and ignoring Him, that just blows me away and nobody can take that from me. The grace of God forgives all my sins and still He wants me to be one of His children, that gives me such joy. At the end of the day, regardless of how life goes, I have that inner peace which money cannot buy and that makes me praise the Lord. I am so excited and delighted by the spirit of the Lord.

He is a Christian and happy, wow! A big happy clap for that! This world is a big melting pot of people, a kaleidoscope of cultures and colours. We should rejoice in the way our Heavenly Father has created us all to be made in His image, yet all so different. You can even see that from the differences in the way we Christians are, Presbyterian, Pentecostal, Anglican, Catholic, charismatic, quite a mix. Is it important that we worship differently or is God just happy we worship?

> Worship should be about what we can give to God, not what He can give us. The Holy Spirit sometimes moves in ways we can't understand, therefore we should never try to limit or restrict Him with one style of worship or praise. The body of Christ is a worldwide church and I can't see why we don't just enjoy these differences. I think if we can only worship God if the keyboards or drums are played a certain way then we need to examine ourselves. We have to be open to Him with our hearts, or He will bypass our church anyway and go to another where they are worshipping in spirit and truth.

Richard Rufus has been happy to take a stand for Jesus. Does he think the Lord has finished changing him or will he be called to be any more different?

> The time I say that He is finished with me I will be in trouble. I'm learning more and more from Him daily. Often His Word brings me an experience of excitement, revelation, hope, peace and encouragement, which He confirms in my spirit. The Holy Spirit is revealing things as I come to know and trust Him more and He won't stop changing me until I meet Him in heaven and He says 'Well done, my good and faithful servant.'

From meeting this incredible, enthusiastic, faith-filled disciple of the Lord, I have absolutely no doubt God will say that, as well as rejoice in His child who has worked hard for His kingdom. (Richard's passion for Jesus certainly makes you want more for yourself!) We are different, He has made each one of us unique and the really exciting thing is He doesn't want this to be an elite little club of churchly buddies. He wants the whole world to be in our gang and by our being 'set apart', He wants us to bring our friends in too, so let's get going and make a difference for Him.

Further Scripture reading

Ephesians 5 v8
For you were once darkness, but now you are light in the Lord. Live as children of light...

Ephesians 4 vs22–24
You were taught, with regard to your former way of life, to put off your old self, which is being corrupted by its deceitful desires; to be made new in the attitude of your minds; and to put on the new self, created to be like God in true righteousness and holiness.

Romans 8 v1–2
Therefore, there is now no condemnation for those who are in Christ Jesus, because through Christ Jesus the law of the Spirit of life set me free from the law of sin and death.

John 15 v8
This is to my Father's glory, that you bear much fruit, showing yourselves to be my disciples.

Joshua 1 v9
Be strong and courageous. Do not be terrified; do not be discouraged, for the Lord your God will be with you wherever you go.

Juan Sara

Photograph courtesy of Sportsfile, Dublin

DATE OF BIRTH: 13.10.78

POSITION: Forward

CLUB HISTORY: Many in South America and Europe

BEST EVER FOOTBALL MOMENT: There are two; 1) In Paraguay when I scored an important goal in a big competition in front of 60,000 people and 2) When I scored a hat-trick in the local derby game for Dundee against Dundee United.

BEST EVER SPIRITUAL MOMENT: Accepting Jesus Christ as my Lord and Saviour.

FAVOURITE ALL-TIME FOOTBALL ELEVEN (*4/4/2 formation*):

		Kahn		
Cafu	Baresi		Pasarella	Roberto Carlos
Pele	Zico		Zidane	Maradona
	Romario		Ronaldo	

FAVOURITE PIECE OF SCRIPTURE: There are so many, but here are three; **Ephesians 3 v16, John 3 v16 and Matthew 11 v28,** *Come to me all you who are weary and burdened and I will give you rest.*

Juan Sara
The devil

Christians worldwide wake up every morning with great intentions, but by the time our feet have hit the floor we've often blown it! Yup, that nasty, little swipe at our brother or sister, shouting huffily back at the parent who is trying to get us to where we want to be on time, swearing under our breath as we stub our toe on the trainers we left lying – sound familiar? While these little lapses of 'niceness' are hardly the crimes of the century, they aren't the way God wants us to live. He knows where they lead. It would be handy to blame others, but often it is just plain old human nature, which sucks. However, what we Christians have to be aware of is that, apart from our own sinful ways, there is someone intent on leading us away from God, someone intent on destroying our faith, and that's the devil. Yes, he does exist, although sightings of an inch-high man with horns, greasy black hair, hooved feet and a tail are rare. So who exactly is the devil and why does he bother with Christians? Answering these questions and more on 'the enemy' is former Dundee Football Club's Argentinian striker, Juan Sara. So who does he think this devil guy is?

> He is a fallen angel, who was once in heaven. The Bible tells us he exists and that he wants to be all-powerful like God. He's intent on destroying God's people and he is both powerful and dangerous.

Okay, he sounds pretty real and a little nasty to me! Juan has been a Christian since he found God as a player in Paraguay.

> I went to Paraguay after playing in Argentina and the Czech Republic. I had the chance to play for a huge club and it was a big challenge. People think football is easy, but it never is and I found it very difficult to perform well. There was pressure from the fans, the manager and journalists and I really didn't handle it very well; my football was not so good. I tried lots of silly things in Paraguay to try and help me, like going to a fortune-teller to find out about my future, but of course, that didn't work. One of my teammates started to talk to me about Jesus, about his faith and the Bible, so I started to read it. Then I went to church to hear more about God and I knew it was real so I accepted Jesus into my life there and then.

Wow, sounds like Juan turned to God just when he needed Him most, right in the middle of a mess! Playing football as a kid on the streets of Argentina was one thing, but to reach the heights he has, did Juan ever dream he would be so successful?

> I always dreamed I would become a footballer and I am so happy that it's happened. I know that it's only one in hundreds who make it to play professionally, so I give God thanks that I have been so fortunate.

Juan Sara obviously has natural ability as well as a burning desire to succeed but where has God been in his career? Does he think that God has guided him this far or is it just down to his own talents?

> It's definitely God. Before I became a Christian I couldn't cope with the pressure and I couldn't give 100 percent. When I became a Christian, however, God gave me His peace and serenity, helping me to leave it all in His hands. He says in the Bible 'Come to me all you who are weak and heavy laden, for I will give you rest'. I find that He can cope with everything, He is Almighty, so I can leave it all to Him. Now the pressure doesn't bother me so much as I know that God will take care of everything.

So Juan's career has hit the heights, but it has also hit some lows, when scoring seems impossible (never good for a striker!). How does he cope when his football isn't going according to plan?

It's really difficult. On occasions when I'm not playing as often as I would like, I always believe God has a plan for me. If He allows these things to happen then I believe it's for a good reason and when you come through it your faith has been strengthened. I have to trust Him when my football is in a difficult stage.

Juan relies on God then to bring him through. A couple of seasons ago he returned from Coventry, from a loan spell. Was he happy to be back at Dundee and did he feel disappointed he wasn't playing down south?

I played only three games and scored one goal for Coventry then I was injured and out for three months. It was very disappointing, I've had a hard time with injuries over the last year and a half and I always ask God, 'Why'? I think the devil doesn't want me to be witnessing about my faith but I always remain faithful. One day I will know why these things have happened, but now I can only turn to God and keep on praising Him.

Juan obviously trusts that God has a good plan for his life, believing He will provide everything Juan needs, hmmm. If it's so simple with God, how does the devil get into our lives then, what ways does the enemy use to attack Christians?

The enemy is always there and I think he tries to take us away from God. I look at a man called Job in the Bible, he had and then lost everything. I think the devil wants to come and take what I have, what God has given me. I know God will guide me; He will be with me in everything. I think the devil attacks us more when we are doing more with God, or for Him. I'm very involved in my church plus I have started to study at college and the devil is definitely there. If we're not being effective for God then he doesn't bother with us.

We have to be in no doubt then, that as we grow in our Christian faith we will also become more of a target for the devil, certainly more likely to encounter him. If we aren't walking with God, the devil won't bother walking with us. Sometimes it can sound a bit scary; the enemy, evil spirits, darkness should we be afraid, isn't it all a bit overwhelming? After all, becoming a Christian looked all nice and sweet in Sunday school.

> I thought it was all about nice, gentle things when I first became a Christian, now I know it's not just like that, the devil is real. We should never be afraid though because we have the Almighty on our side and His Holy Spirit within us. He gives us the tools we need, to stop the devil's attacks, He is always there too.

So, we have the power of our Almighty God, creator of the universe, King of Kings, Lord of all at our disposal, hmmm, perhaps we have nothing to fear after all! Many of us have made the mistake of thinking that sin and evil are simply the stuff that really bad guys do. You know, murder, violence, torture and the like, therefore, our little white lies and fights with family or friends don't really count – *wrong*! While we're unlikely to go to jail for making a fool of the class loner's latest hairstyle(!), God hates the pain and humiliation we heap on others. It's often into the little things, the odd bad word and feeling, that the devil pops his ugly head, after all if he can persuade you to keep on pulling just a little away from God, who knows how far he can take you? Juan is a guy who has a lot of blessings in his life, how does he guard against letting the enemy in, giving him a chance to turn him from God?

> Pray. I feel that when I get involved with church and fellowship I am stronger. When I meet other Christians we speak the same language, we're brothers in Christ. Praying, fellowship and studying His Word are the main ways to defeat the devil when he comes into our lives. I'm much stronger in my faith when I'm doing these things and getting closer to God. Football can be a difficult world to be in, if I don't do these things then that's when its easier for the devil to get into my life, to try and keep me further from God.

The devil may be doing his best to trap you and trick you, but never forget he is already beaten. Jesus took him on and won. The power of the resurrection is that Jesus defeated death and the devil will be completely obliterated on Jesus' return, the second coming, so we know that the victory is ours, yeehah! The devil is already a loser; he is soon to be history too! For Juan, and for most of us, one way the enemy works is by tempting us. After all, if he did come to try and destroy our faith and our lives in a cloud of black smoke with blood red eyes and ten-inch nails, he would be easier to spot and therefore easier to resist. No, he's a bit smarter than that and uses things and people we love, our weaknesses and our past to try to keep us back from God's blessings, nasty little creep! How do we deal with this then, how do we recognise the areas he works in our lives?

> Sometimes it's difficult to recognise him, but we do have the Bible. We can go to it and discover if the thoughts, words or actions we have are good or bad. That's why we should study His Word because we can be armed with His truth against the devil.

Playing professional football must open plenty of doors and not all of them good ones. Has Juan's career made it even harder to resist the devil, after all, temptations must be in plentiful supply!

> The football world is difficult; there are plenty of temptations. I think in my case God has strengthened me to deal with it. I try and look for the good opportunities my profession brings as I can be a witness in many places because I play football. I'm able to get into churches and meetings and share my faith. I don't drink so that's no problem and I'm always with my wife when I go out. However God says that He always provides a way out when we do get tempted or are put in a difficult situation. I really believe His Spirit has guided me through any temptations.

So praying, Bible reading and thinking practically are a must in this battle! The Bible has plenty to say about how we should live our lives and even more about how God loves us. Perhaps we need to really get a handle on this, *God loves us so much, he loves us just as much as He loved Jesus, He made us to love us, wow!* So when we know how much God loves us, we shouldn't worry too much about the devil, after all, we are on the winning side. However, the devil often likes us to believe that we are never going to experience this and that we've blown it – HE IS A LIAR! Nothing we can do, however bad, can separate us from God's love. If we truly believe, and if we are sorry for the sin, we are always forgiven if we take it to God. It's not always easy to let go if we have done something wrong though and often the devil can keep reminding us of it, telling us we are still bad, how do we learn to ignore him, learn to trust God for forgiveness?

> We have to look at the cross. When Jesus died He took all our sins and everything we have done wrong. We all make mistakes, we are only human, but God says He has already forgiven us. We have to try and live as God wants, closer to Him, but always remember Jesus has paid the price for us. The good thing is we can pray, ask forgiveness and He will give it. He doesn't want us to be separate from Him because of anything we do. You can ask Him to guide you and help you give up something that's bad, after all, His Spirit is within us helping us along.

Football is a sport which millions worldwide love and it can be a wonderful spectacle, plus a fantastic arena to bring people together. However, it's also a place that the devil plays, using this beautiful game to cause intense rivalry and bitterness, not to mention worshipping false idols! How does Juan see it, has the devil stolen this sport for himself, or can it be used to further God's kingdom?

> I think the devil is definitely in the football world, in all sorts of places. We as Christians have to be an example then, standing up for what we believe and living our lives for God. We as Christians have to be the ones to change football. The world is full of sin, it's everywhere and perhaps football is worse because of all the money in the sport. The devil has

certainly used the game for his purposes, but we can use football for the Kingdom Of God by being a good witness for Him. It's amazing how many Christians are appearing in the sport – look at all the Brazilians after they won the World Cup with a message about Jesus on their shirts. Even the biggest teams need to have God on their side.

Speaking of shirts (well, Juan was) when did Juan start his own 'Scripture show' after each goal?

In Paraguay, I saw other players doing the same thing and I thought it was a good idea. I love doing it because it gives me another chance to share my faith.

Of course one of the ways the enemy loves to see us move away from God is when we replace Him in our lives, put something else in the number one spot. For so many, a footballer can become an idol, especially a world-famous one like Maradona. Despite all Maradona's difficulties, does Juan recognise this is a problem?

It's difficult because anything we put before God is an idol. I always want to put God first in my life, as it's the only way I feel happy. I know some people may put me in a higher place in their lives because of football, but I have to just try and show them through my witnessing that it's God who's important, not Juan Sara.

A big raspberry to Satan then, looks like this is another battle he is losing. We're not all extremely talented footballers (shame), so for many of us, trying to find our heart's desires, our roles in life, can be a heap of trouble. Which exams to take, how to discover our talents (if they aren't easy to spot), how to get confidence if we lack it, how to handle making difficult choices? Sometimes the world just seems so big and, quite frankly, difficult. How do we keep ourselves on top of things and stop the devil from getting in when we are confused and need to think clearly?

I think the best way is praying, again God will always guide you to do His will. Being involved in church life and meeting other Christians is good and it helps you to feel His Spirit inside you, helping you make any decision. He always provides you with guidance if you turn to Him.

Just trust God! Life as a Christian may not always be easy, but it's certainly never dull. God is bringing us on a journey back to Him and as we find Him we also discover such peace and happiness we cannot begin to imagine – excellent! It's a little annoying that the purpose of the devil seems to be to destroy this for us; however, we have to be aware of it. The devil may be crafty enough to trick us and lie to us, he may cause us to suffer unnecessary pain and heartache, but we mustn't give up, God has provided an escape route for us, we *can* get rid of the devil. Eh, how?

I find the way to defeat the devil is to always be seeking God and His will. I find it easier to hear from God when I am worshipping Him and learning from His Word. I have people I can turn to; this is a key to fighting the battle. I can pray with them, share what my weaknesses are and we can all encourage one another. God really blessed me in Scotland with people I can have good fellowship with, people I trust and who answer my questions.

Bring it on then, we have the armour and backing of God! Juan Sara has plenty of time yet on the pitch, this talented Argentinian has even more to come. However, when the football is over, what does he see himself doing, will it be back to South America?

I'm not sure but I'm praying about it. Sometimes it's difficult to imagine another way of life, but I know He will guide me. At the moment He has called me to study His Word at college so I'm sure He has a plan for me. All I am certain of, is that it will be a good one, that's what the Bible tells me.

Life is an adventure to be enjoyed as well as endured. Football is just a part of Juan's life; God is the centre of it all! The devil may come to try and persuade you to give up on God, but don't worry, God never gives up on you. If you've acted or reacted wrongly, confess it to God, forgive yourself and the other person, then move on. Don't let the devil keep you in a place filled with guilt and remorse; you are a child of God. The more you feel under attack, the more you must be doing for God, just keep on doing good and God will keep on doing God. As you would expect, the devil is absolutely terrified of the power of God's Word, and of prayer, so keep on using these tools. Drugs, drink, violence, sexual abuse, depravity and greed seem to be the tools of the devil's trade, hmmm, it's getting easier to spot him! Can we really ever be totally 'devil free'? Can we get rid of the little pest forever or do we have to battle constantly?

> It's a constant struggle, Romans says it's a battle in the mind so we have to fill our minds with the things of God. It can be difficult because as we know the devil is trying to pull us away from God but if we keep on doing the things like prayer and Bible study, we can get closer to God. I really only feel completely happy when I am filled with His Spirit.

Juan Sara is someone who has to keep turning to God to get rid of the devil. His faith and his football mean he can be used to bring glory to God, so why does the devil not just give up, can't he see that Juan loves the Lord, why does he persist?

> He doesn't want us to tell others about Christ, he wants us to be bad examples for others. It can be difficult to be a constant witness for Christ as people are just waiting for any mistake. I took a decision to give my life to God. Having everyone watch my life is something I can do for Him, give a little back after everything He has given me.

Players like Juan and those featured in this book are targets for God's enemy, the devil, because he knows they can reach hundreds and thousands of people with their story, please pray for them.

So Juan has a fabulous career, fabulous talent, life is sweet, but unfortunately it's not like that for all of us. For some, it seems all of the devil's plans are succeeding and we have to face loneliness, illness, death of loved ones, abuse and psychological problems. How do we cope, how do we battle the enemy in a place where it seems he holds the aces?

This life is not the main thing; we're going to have eternal life with God. We're going to suffer here at times but we have to remember that we will live one day with God and everything will be fantastic. Even when times are difficult and everything is going wrong, I try to hold onto the fact that one day this will be over and a new life in heaven will begin. Our troubles on earth never last forever either, God wants to bless us so we must just hang on to Him.

Fear not then, the devil may bug you a lot, but we have the assurance of victory and of our place in eternity to look forward to. Funny isn't it, the more you turn to God's Word and trust in His power and plans for you, the more the devil becomes annoyed. However, the more you trust God and let Him lead you, the further away from the devil you go. So long to the devil – God says: 'So long, you're red-carded and sent for an early bath!'

Further Scripture reading

I John 3 v8
He who does what is sinful is of the devil, because the devil has been sinning from the beginning. The reason the Son of God appeared was to destroy the devil's work.

Ephesians 4 v26–27
'In your anger do not sin': Do not let the sun go down while you are still angry, and do not give the devil a foothold.

1 Peter 5 vs8–9
Be self-controlled and alert. Your enemy the devil prowls around like a roaring lion looking for someone to devour. Resist him, standing firm in the faith, because you know that your brothers throughout the world are undergoing the same kind of sufferings.

John 8 v44
When he (the devil) lies, he speaks his native language, for he is a liar and the father of lies.

Graeme Mathie

DATE OF BIRTH: 17.10.82

POSITION: Defender

CLUB HISTORY: Coventry City, AFC Bournemouth, Motherwell, East Fife, Albion Rovers

INTERNATIONAL HISTORY: Under-16, Under-18 and Under-20 caps for Scotland

BEST EVER FOOTBALL MOMENT: Wearing the dark blue of Scotland is always special and even though it was only at youth team level it was still an honour to play for my country.

BEST EVER SPIRITUAL MOMENT: Being baptised on 17/08/03. It was a great day. It is scriptural when we are baptised, it not only signifies the washing away of sins, but I really felt a complete opening up to God. Since then I have been through some struggles in my life, including not playing due to injury and the thought of my contract finishing at the end of the season, but I have an absolute peace in my heart and I know God is with me, and has a plan and purpose for my life. Also, seeing my best friend give his life to the Lord. It's such a special feeling when God uses you to bring others into His Kingdom.

God's never offside

Jesus (always saves!)

Noah (soaks up floods of attack!), God (the rock!), Samson (strength and aerial prowess!), Daniel (left-back in the den, but defeated the lions)

John the Baptist (prepares the way!), Paul (spreads it about well!), Abraham (covers great distances!), Moses (a great leader!)

David (for his striking ability with the stone!), Adam (first to everything, but prone to falling!)

Subs:

Thomas (doubts his ability!)

Zacchaeus (unpopular!)

Judas (can't be trusted!)

FAVOURITE PIECE OF SCRIPTURE: **Jeremiah 29 vs11–13**. A footballer's life can be very insecure. There is a lot of moving around between clubs, and it always helps to know that my times are in God's hands. No matter what I come up against, either in my spiritual life or my career, God is there with me and has a plan for my life that nothing or no-one can change.

Graeme Mathie
No sex before marriage

Graeme Mathie is a 22-year-old Celtic Football Club community development officer and defender with Albion Rovers, presently in the Scottish 3rd Division. His professional career began at Coventry at the age of 16, which saw him spend a very unhappy 18 months learning his trade. Marooned in the midst of a regime based on hard talking, hard tackling and hard hearts, Graeme lost some of his confidence, shying away from the ball on the pitch. Disillusioned perhaps but never despairing, Graeme had to draw deep on his spiritual resources after the experience opened his eyes to the world of football and the world in general. You sense however, aside from his work, God used him at Coventry. This dark period has actually enhanced Graeme's determination and commitment, for God moves in mysterious ways. A happier period was to follow, when at 17, Graeme moved for one season to Bournemouth. This was a time of prosperity, both football-wise and also spiritually. It was also a time for, modelling, yes, modelling! Graeme was entered by the team physio into a national magazine's Eligible Bachelor Competition and soon found himself at photo shoots and being interviewed on national television. Naturally for Graeme his faith was something he talked about. Sex before marriage was something he was asked about a lot at the time and here he is again, doing a whole chapter – doesn't God move in mysterious ways!

A return to Scotland beckoned and he signed for Motherwell in 2002 where he missed a lot of play following a serious cruciate injury. He has gone to church for most of his life and became a Christian at the age of 14. He is a great witness for the Lord, keen churchgoer, extremely engaging character and a *virgin*, yep, I said virgin! Obviously this means he is weird with a distinct lack of social skills and charm, right? Wrong! Graeme is perfectly normal, healthy, handsome, funny, talented, (did I say normal?), yet he is completely committed to saying 'No' to sex until he is married. This was not a difficult decision he made, it's just part of his faith

> I don't think it was a conscious decision at 13 or 14, I wasn't really aware of it at the time. When I was on youth football trips other people would talk about it but to be honest I didn't know that much about sex and it certainly wasn't something I was ready for. However, because sex is all around us I think this is one thing that separates Christians from non-Christians. I would certainly stick by the 'no sex before marriage' issue and now it is a conscious decision I have taken.

Graeme was like many kids growing up, part of a family who certainly knew about God without necessarily knowing Him personally.

> I've gone to church ever since I can remember. I think church was very much a Sunday thing, very traditional, about moral teachings and trying to live as good a life as possible but that's all there was to it. It wasn't until secondary school when an RE teacher asked me if I was saved, if I was going to heaven? When I said I thought so as I had been pretty good he pointed out that it wasn't about that and I should go read **John 3 v16**, and find out what being a Christian is really about. Nobody had ever spoken the truth to me like that before and I went away and read more, really got into the gospel and I started to realise there was so much to it.

Because of this Graeme changed churches to one with a more lively style of worship and really opened his eyes and his heart to God, asking Jesus into his life as his friend and saviour.

It wasn't the road to Damascus experience I thought it would be. My uncle had a very powerful conversion when he saw visions and really felt God speak to him but I just asked God into my life and that was it. Although I think I did it on my knees with one eye opened half expecting the big, dramatic event to happen, I kept saying to people, 'Am I missing something, what else do I have to do?' But it's not like that for everyone, it's as simple and as difficult as inviting Jesus into your life.

Simple or difficult to ask the Lord in is one thing, sticking to your new-found convictions can be quite another, especially when refraining from sex is one of them. How did he explain this to friends?

Most of them knew right from the start and of course some of them used to take the mickey out of me for it, some still do. In fact, just recently, Dylan Kerr, another professional footballer, met me in Troon town centre and was shouting at me across the street, 'How's the injury?' I told him it was getting better. 'Are you still modelling?' I told him I wasn't and then he shouted right across the street, 'Are you still a virgin?' unfazed I just said: 'Yeah, I am!' It's brilliant. I have friends who are virgins, all in the same age group as me, they just have not met the right person and have decided to wait.

Explaining to a bunch of your close friends who share your beliefs is one thing, but what about when Graeme had a girlfriend, wasn't it a nightmare putting this into practice, especially if she wasn't a Christian?

My first serious girlfriend was when I was 14 and she was 16. She had said she didn't want to 'do' anything till I was 16, so I thought fine, I've got a couple of years to worry about it, but that fizzled out after a few months. However, when I was 16, I had a 15-year-old girlfriend and early on in the relationship I told her that sex before marriage was out for me and that if it was an issue we should just part now before things got serious. She was happy about it at the time but towards the end of our relationship it did become a problem. We dated for about two years and during that time a lot of her friends started having sexual relationships and were quite open about it. She was one of the few people who wasn't having sex and that was difficult for her as she used to say things like, 'You don't really love me if you don't want to sleep with me'. The relationship could only go one of two ways, either she was the girl for me and we should talk marriage or she was not and we should end it and this is what happened, we stopped seeing each other.

So does this desire to stay pure until you're married mean you have to stay away from people you are attracted to, lessening the temptations?

When I was young I always thought if you were going to go out with a Christian girl she was going to be ugly and I would just have to put up with it. Most of the girls I was attracted to when I was a teenager had really short skirts, long blonde hair and didn't go to church. Now I know that's rubbish! I have gone out with some attractive girls but after a while you look for more than just looks in a relationship, although obviously there has to be an attraction.

Not only has Graeme found an attractive girl he can relate to, she has agreed to marry him! That's right, the super cool Mr M has broken hearts all over Ayrshire (he asked me to write this part!) by finding Miss Wonderful in the shape of the very beautiful Miss Joanne Ross (she's too sweet to ask me to write that part!). So how did this happen?

I met Joanne at a church ceilidh and didn't know her very well at all. I was still recovering from a knee injury at the time and so my chat up line was, 'I can't do the fast ones so we'll have to slow dance together'. After a couple of dances we swapped numbers, texted each other the next day, then agreed to meet up. At first the attraction was physical, I think she is absolutely gorgeous, but as I got to know her I realised there was so much more to her, so much on the inside. I think that's why the relationship is so strong to this day, although I am attracted to her looks, we are definitely connected on more than one level.

So take heart, there are attractive Christians in the world! Does this mean that we should only have relationships with other Christians or does it not really make any difference if we are not having sex anyway?

The first girl I dated who was a Christian was so different. It's certainly easier when you are with someone who understands and shares your beliefs, particularly on this subject. We can both help each other to stay faithful to God and there is a lot less pressure. Girls I have gone out with before have had sexual relationships with others and it was something I had to think about. The guys in the dressing room used to ask if I wanted to date a virgin and when I said, 'Yes,' they said I was looking for a needle in a haystack. Sometimes I used to feel really bad, really judgemental when I was seeing a girl who had had sexual relations with others. If they asked me if it bothered me, I had to be honest and say, 'Yes, yes it did,' because I can't lie about how I feel. There was a girl I really liked who had had sex before, but she started to come to church with me, really showed a desire to find God. I was confused because I had feelings for her but I also knew it bothered me she had been with other people. Through prayer and guidance in the church, people explained to me that God could restore anything and wipe away the sins of the past, and that He could restore her. However, the relationship faded away and I realise it wasn't meant to be.

For many people, the idea of waiting until marriage for sex is a ridiculous one, after all, why did God give us all these feelings and hormones in the first place? Why does Graeme think God wants us to wait, isn't that a bit cruel or is it a test?

If you believe in God, then you also believe in another force at work. I think sometimes the devil puts these things in your way. You can look at sex in a couple of ways, first, just as an act to be enjoyed, pure and simple or from a spiritual point of view. I believe sex is an act where two people come together as one, what God has made, let no man separate and I think that for sex as well as marriage. God made it to be a joining together of two bodies in the sexual act and I think that's the similarity, that's what God intends and that's not cruel. I know a few friends who are waiting for that someone special and for me I find things like heavy petting become less special if you do it with everyone. What could be more special than saving this for the person you want to spend the rest of your life with.

God may have seen the benefits of waiting till we have met our life partner and committing to marriage before we have sex, but what about the devil, isn't Satan having a field day with our physical urges and how can we ignore them?

That's the thing the boys want to ask me about all the time, sex before marriage! They always ask me, 'Surely you want to, surely you think about it?' My answer is always, 'Yes, I'm a Christian, not a perfect saint!' You have these urges, of course, and I think it is a very easy thing for Satan to get a hold of, after all, sex is all around us. In the dressing room there is every kind of paper, some with 'Page Three' or similar, and when someone is reading it there is the temptation to have a look too, but when you realise this is wrong and a distraction you have to stop and think, no, that's not for me. It's very difficult not to get caught up in the way the world is, not to watch the films or read the magazines and just because it's accessible, doesn't make it right. I find it helpful to think about the whole lust and sex issue as like being on a cliff top and asking yourself the question: Where are you going to put your barrier? If you put your barrier too close to the edge there is a chance you will fall, if it's further away from the edge, there is less chance of you falling. It might just be a wee look at 'Page Three' one day, a book or magazine the next and where does it stop? You have to have it within yourself to say no. It is a slippery slope and you don't want to get involved in it, because sex is so accessible.

So we must try and avoid the movies, magazines, websites etc, which arouse us and seek a more Godly worldview. Does that mean we should be dressing accordingly, you know, girls in yashmaks and boys in head-to-toe baggy black? Are we actually falling into the sin trap if we want to look good?

I don't really think there is any need for that! Certainly there are some people who dress very provocatively and there has to be a happy medium. There is a balance between looking good and not making yourself look like something you don't want to promote. I think it's fine to want to look good, perfectly natural. God cares about the way you look, He made you and He loves you, why wouldn't He want you to look the best you can? Just because we are Christians doesn't mean we can't try and look good.

Life is meant to be enjoyed, but it does seem a pity to allow the devil and our own weaknesses to rob us of a beautiful blessing that God has carefully and lovingly created for us. Hmm, this saying 'No' to sex until marriage might actually be worth it! So, if we do decide sex is for marriage and we are determined to steer clear of the temptations we know can ensnare us, what can we do to help us resist, where does Graeme turn for guidance?

Prayer! I would say every time I go and meet with my fiancée we just pray that His will is done. Read Scripture about it, pray together and pray in church. God is my guidance and He sometimes puts a leaning on one of our hearts when we are together, just to say no, let's stop things just now, it's not right for us at this time, so prayer really helps.

So, getting prayerful helps when we get tempted, but so does getting practical. Like Graeme says, you have to put your own barriers up – if the Channel 5 movie makes you think about sex don't watch it. Does going to the club and having a few drinks make it harder to stop at just a kiss? Then stop having those drinks, the devil is always trying to tempt us, but God always gives us a way out. If you're tempted a lot don't feel bad – Jesus was tempted too, see **Matthew 4 vs1–11**, he quoted God's Word and made the devil flee, hmmm, perhaps reading the Bible might also help (see Chapter 4!).

Praying, Bible study, good mates and being practical may be fine and helpful to those who have not had sex yet, but what if we already have, does this mean we might as well keep on having sex, after all, we have spoiled it now?

> I wouldn't have thought so! When we talk about sex, it's a gift from God to be enjoyed. I know unmarried Christian couples who have felt it a burden to stop having sex, having had it before and been at that level of intimacy. However, they've stopped. I imagine it would take a lot of prayer, really seeking His will, but when you have told a lie you don't just keep on lying because you have done it, you try not to do it again. I guess it would be really difficult, but that's why prayer is so important, let Him give you the strength to stop until it's the right time.

For some today sex can seem like an answer to prayer, a chance to get intimate with someone, a chance to stop being alone. For others, it can seem like the only answer, the only way to hold onto a loved partner who is wanting to sleep together. How would Graeme advise those who truly believe they are in love, yet know they will lose this person if they don't have sex with them?

> The easiest thing is to say, just split up, they are not the one for you, but at the time this is the hardest thing to do. If you really believe you are in love with someone, nowadays the physical side of things is such a big deal. I am so glad to be in a relationship where that side of it is just taken away. When I had to deal with it in the past though, it was very, very, difficult. I had to stay true to my beliefs. If you feel you are in love you

can become blind to things and I would say, once again, you really need to pray and seek what is important. I don't believe that someone who loves you would make you do something like that. Even without a Christian viewpoint it's quite a big commitment to make and I certainly wouldn't advise anyone to rush into it.

Losing the wrong person because we are not having sex doesn't seem like such a bad idea anyway! Life in God's will can be a tricky place to navigate and we often need the support of good friends and fellow Christians. Has Graeme been fortunate in having people around him to support his wish to remain a virgin and has he ever needed to lean on them? Or is this a very private issue, unlike healing, for example?

That was the one thing which came up time and time again for me after that bachelor competition. I said on television during an interview that I was a virgin, I wanted to remain one until my marriage and a few people were shocked. I discovered lots of people in my church began praying for me, believing I had set myself up for an attack from Satan. I don't really go to people and ask for guidance, I am happy that my fiancée understands and shares my beliefs. Although it really helps to be accountable to other people, sometimes when people ask us about these things, it helps us to be more aware of the boundaries.

Okay, this is all great advice if you fancy someone of the opposite sex but what if you're attracted to someone of the same sex, how would we deal with this?

I don't think the church deals with this very well. Some churches are far too judgemental and come down really hard on homosexuals, others have ceremonies where gay people are married. I find both these approaches very hard to deal with. Believing in a God who made Adam and Eve, for a man and a woman to come together to create new life, this is a very difficult issue. I think it must be very hard for anyone who is a

Christian to struggle with this, but you must really pray about it, I know I say that for everything, but it's the truth, turn to God and let Him guide you. It's a trick that the evil one uses, to try and keep you from the truth and from God's blessings and if we can understand that and pray about it we can get in touch with God.

Perhaps one paragraph in this book can't answer every question on this difficult subject, but don't give up on God. If you're dealing with homosexual desires find a Christian you *really* trust and chat with them or try speaking to a Christian counsellor in confidence. Don't let anybody condemn you – God doesn't.

In today's world, keeping our virginity or avoiding sex till marriage would definitely set us apart, which is exactly why we are called to be *in* the world, but not *of* it. How are we supposed to deal with our friends who don't have our convictions?

The dressing room is notorious for it; a lot of the banter is sexually orientated. Sometimes I think because the guys know my beliefs they don't want to talk to me about it. Sometimes you sit and listen to them and just think, oh dear what is this like, and I actually despair of some of the things that are going on. I don't join in although I can still accept it as banter in the dressing room. Sometimes they will have a laugh with me, ask if I saw my girlfriend last night and then ask at what time. They say things like, 'Yeah, she had to leave mine early to get to yours!' I don't bother about it, they know what I believe in and I think that makes me a bit different but certainly not isolated. They don't talk about sex all the time, so I join in again when it comes round to football or something else. Some of my friends and I were sitting with a female friend of theirs who is sexually active and she began boasting about how good it was, how she couldn't understand how we could still be virgins at 20 and 21. My friend just said to her, 'We can be like you any time we want, but you can never be like us again!' I thought that was a really good way of looking at it. You have to stay true to what you believe in, God made sex to be a pleasure in His timing.

Not everyone can make the choice when to lose their virginity or explore their sexual desires within a loving marriage as sexual abuse can rob them of that decision and inflict much pain, sadness, guilt (wrongly) and shame. If you've been abused, molested, touched or made to see, hear or experience anything sexual you did not choose, there is *no* condemnation in Christ. Jesus came to earth to heal the broken hearts and I believe he weeps with you. What you have experienced may have traumatised you but it need not destroy you. Ask Jesus to come and pour His love into the areas of your heart and memory that hurt you. The journey to wholeness may be a long slow one or may happen overnight, but you can find peace, love, acceptance and restoration in Christ. An abuser cannot take your purity. Christian counselling may help or a book on the subject from a Christian bookstore – Jesus will not leave you in pain, He promises beauty from ashes in **Isaiah 61 vs1–3**.

Graeme Mathie may be 'set apart' from others because he has stuck to his beliefs, but you can be sure God has very special blessings in store for him. Graeme has to be braver than most of us because he is in such a high profile worldly arena, but isn't it a fantastic encouragement to know there are people like him who are not weird and loners, just committed Christians who have a heart to remain pure for God and for their future partners. I take my hat off to him and ask you to keep him in your prayers, the guy is a star!

Our Heavenly Father has designed us to be able to say no, we just need to trust Him and cover ourselves in prayer as we journey through life. It may seem like temptation is everywhere and you are alone in this constant battle, but God will reward you, not just in heaven, but here on earth because when you do meet the right person, what joy!

Further Scripture reading

I Corinthians 6 v13
The body is not meant for sexual immorality, but for the Lord, and the Lord for the body.

Romans 1 v24
Therefore God gave them over in the sinful desires of their hearts to sexual impurity for the degrading of their bodies with one another. They exchanged the truth of God for a lie, and worshipped and served created things rather than the Creator – who is to be praised forever. Amen.

1 Corinthians 6 v18
Flee from sexual immorality. All other sins a man commits are outside his body, but he who sins sexually sins against his own body.

Romans 1 v27
Men committed indecent acts with other men, and received in themselves the due penalty for their perversion.

Cyril Regis

DATE OF BIRTH: 09.02.58

POSITION: Forward

CLUB HISTORY: Haynes 1977, West Bromwich Albion 1977–84, Coventry City 1984–89, Aston Villa 1991–93, Wolves 1993–94, Wycombe Wanderers 1994–95, Chester City 1995–96

INTERNATIONAL HISTORY: Full caps for England caps

BEST EVER FOOTBALL MOMENT: Winning the FA Cup with Coventry in 1987 at Wembley.

BEST EVER SPIRITUAL MOMENT: When Jesus became a reality.

FAVOURITE ALL-TIME FOOTBALL ELEVEN (*4/4/2 formation*):

			Schmeichel			
Roberto Carlos		Baresi		Beckenbauer		Maldini
	Best		Cruyff		Maradona	Zidane
		Pele			Ronaldo	

FAVOURITE PIECE OF SCRIPTURE: **Galatians 2 v20**

Cyril Regis
How to handle God's gifts

Okay, so we're now aware that God created us in His image and He is pretty special, therefore, so are we – excellent!

We are loved, cherished, wanted, needed, cleansed, forgiven, basically sorted in Christ, does it mean we are perfect? Obviously not or everyone would be able to play for Ayr United!

Seriously, it can be mighty self-affirming when we realise God has made us unique and has a special plan and purpose solely for us that no one else can have, wow!

It is important to bask in this, to really let it sink in. *You're special, God loves you, He thinks and knows there's no one like you, you're a star, a treasure, a reflection of your Heavenly Father.* These are facts – enjoy.

One thing that can be difficult to deal with is ourselves. Yes, how do you keep a perspective on what is a God-given gift and what is your own talent? After all when life is going well and we're riding high, how do we remain grounded in Him, ready to give Him all the glory? Step up Cyril Regis, a guy obviously enjoying using the talents God has given him and working hard with them. The former West Bromwich Albion legend has now retired from the game, but, despite a successful, illustrious career, he knows having a relationship with God has brought him his real treasures and riches.

I was brought up a Catholic, but about 13 or 14 I turned my back on it, went my own way. It really took the death of my best friend, Laurie Cunningham, in a car crash in 1988 to make me stop, think and ask, 'What's it all about?' Our lives had run on parallel lines, we'd even been in a car crash in Spain a couple of years before he died after drinking and partying too much. It made me think, 'Where is Laurie now? Is there heaven and hell?' One minute he was here, now he's gone and all his riches left behind. I could have died two years ago and the impact of his death made me search for the answers. After about 14 months of looking and going round churches a friend of mine came round to my house and we spoke for about five hours. We talked about loads of things: God's love, forgiveness, the Devil, heaven and hell, how God transforms you, the need to come as you are, the Holy Spirit, everything. I felt I had to give my life to Christ there in my room. So I prayed, 'Lord I don't know if you are there or not, but if you are, come into my life.' I didn't feel anything right away, this was Thursday and by Saturday I was back to my old ways; drinking, womanising and partying till 7 am. By Monday I was back in Birmingham and really conscious that one minute I was asking God into my life, the next I was up to my old tricks. I read a book by Michael Green and I was racked by guilt. There, in my room, I felt His presence, I knew He was with me and I was so touched by Him. From that day on I have tried to walk in His footsteps.

So Cyril has a relationship with God and had a burning desire to be a footballer, one that he obviously realised. What about when he was starting out, does he think God led him into football, was that His plan?

I think God gives you choices. Even in your Christian life, if you make the wrong choice and get off track a bit, He simply guides you gently back to where He wants you to be. He never takes away your free will, but He does have plans.

I had a foundation to build on because of my Catholic

upbringing, but I completely turned my back on that. If I knew there was a seedy story coming out about me in a newspaper, I would get down on my knees and pray that God would sort it for me, promising I wouldn't do it again, but of course when it was over, I was back to my old ways. I might want to change, stop being selfish, hurting people, but that only lasted about a month and I would go back to the old strongholds, my comfort zones. God hates our bad behaviour, but loves us and so He was patient with me when I was going off the rails. Looking back I can see how He guided me into and used my football.

So, panic not if you feel you've got a bit messed up or off track. Cyril was someone God had plans for and all his excessive partying and frolicking might have delayed some blessings but never stopped God's plan to save him. If we discover God's plan for us and realise He has given us the talent to achieve it, can we just sit back and let it happen, after all, nothing can stop the plans of the Almighty? Surely it doesn't require any effort from us?

No, our talent is a seed. He has done so much for us in real terms, he's gone 15 trillion, million miles for us to give us what we want and we just have to take one step. He gives us this seed of talent but to get it to its full fruition it takes Him, you, other people, determination, perseverance, hunger and passion, all these things. They are like sunlight and water to get your seed of talent to its level of perfection or competence.

Okay, so perhaps we need to put some effort in too. Life seldom just goes according to plan, as we've discussed in previous chapters, but when God has equipped us for a particular role, surely it all falls into place more easily? After all, if we have a talent for singing, writing, sport, dance, drama, whatever, does this mean God will open up those particular doors for us?

Through prayer God will guide you. He tells us He will give us the desires of our heart, but often with God there are conditions. Are you in the right place to receive His Blessing, where is your heart? I want the best for my children, but sometimes they are not in the place to receive that. If my three-year-old daughter wanted a beautiful porcelain doll worth hundreds of pounds she wouldn't be in the place to receive it. She wouldn't treasure it, look after it, value it; she would most probably break it. God knows the right time to give us His gifts, we have to trust His timing is perfect.

People who have an obvious talent, like Cyril, are not always the norm. There are far more of us who are average at lots of things or so we think. Remember, God created us in His image, creator of the universe, all-powerful, all-seeing, hmmm, life as a substitute isn't an option! If we accept that God has given everyone talents and gifts (some aren't as obvious as others!) then how do we go about discovering what they are?

It's where the love is! Would you go through the cold for it, stay up all night, give up seeing your friends for it, go through the pain barrier for it, miss TV for it? If you gravitate towards academia, sport, a vocation, whatever, it's where you have a love for it and you will do anything to be doing it or using it. My mum and dad used it as discipline; if I didn't behave then I couldn't play football on a Saturday – it worked. To achieve anything you have to work hard and go through many peaks and troughs, that's why the love and passion for it has to be there.

Once you've discovered what your talents are (yes, you have some, perhaps it's being a good reader!) then get your finger out and use them, eh, if you can be bothered. Discovering what you are good at and what God has made special about you is one thing, but how do you go about making it better? For Cyril training was obviously a way to look after his talent. Is this important in life?

Absolutely! Because God has given you this talent there is a sense of humility, such gratitude, that you should want to look after it. If we let it sit it will fade away, you have to apply yourself. There are certain demands for your talent, certain disciplines, whatever the talent is you have to work hard with it. It's difficult, being a footballer is mental but you have to discipline yourself. When I was 16 or 17 I was playing non-league football. On a Friday night my mates would be going to a party, lots of booze, girls, music, but I would have to say, 'No', I needed to have that strength of mind. Some of those guys were better footballers than me but they never made it professionally because they didn't look after their talents.

So, if your talent is sport: practice, practice, practice, likewise with music, drama, dance or writing. It's also vital to use it whatever it is. If you are good at listening take every opportunity to be there for others, if you are blessed with a cheerful sunny nature (who is?), smile as often as possible at your fellow man, if you are strong use it behind the scenes at church or helping folks to move house, if you can read well why not visit people with poor eyesight and share the Bible with them, whatever you can do, do it often!

So, here we are using our time and our talents, we are all being the best footballers/dancers/singers/farmers/bikers/technicians/swimmers we can be and things are sweet. We know that we are good at sharing our faith and we do, we're playing the lead in the school play, editing the newspaper, singing in a chart-topping band and climbing Mount Everest last Sunday (after the service of course!) – nothing to this. At this point using our talents may be second nature, discovering where we are going is an adventure and searching for our gifts is fun, however, remembering where we got them may be difficult! How does Cyril juggle being good at public speaking and remembering God gave him the gift?

I became a Christian when I was 33 so I had lived a full life in the world. I had had ten or 15 years in the public eye before I truly relied on God and it certainly helped me understand a few things, it was like the pieces of a jigsaw slotting together. I can pass my experiences onto others. Football is important, money is important but once you have God in your life He is *most* important. I was only interested in myself, making money, having lots of sex, stepping over people to get to the top, being the best. God gives you an insight into money though, the church needs it and He wants you to have it. He gave me a perspective on football too. God gives us insight into who He is and that makes us humble. You don't want it to be about selfish or material things, you want it to be about God and how great He is.

It sounds a bit like a juggling act at times God wants us to recognise our gifts, get out there and use them, practice and perfect them, yet always remember that He is the one who created them. How does Cyril keep his feet on the ground? Especially having played for his country and been successful at club level, didn't he get carried away with the praise and adulation, after all, he had thousands of fans cheering him on and letting him know how wonderful he was. Wasn't it easy to forget God and just accept the glory?

When I was at the top it was all me, I was desperate for the fame. However, now I know Him, I want all the glory to go to Him. I know it's not me, anything I'm good at, it's all from Him. Also, you have to recognise all the people God puts round about you to help you achieve. I had a wonderful *landlady* when I first came to Birmingham from London who stopped me from becoming homesick and leaving. My *mother* had no money and had to put cardboard in my shoes just so I could play football. The *manager* who believed in me put an arm around my shoulder and encouraged me when I wasn't scoring goals. When you consider that God has put all these people in place to help and support you, it reminds you how humble you should be. You may have a talent for something but you can be sure others have played a part in helping you succeed.

It's really important then to continue to come before God and give Him the thanks and praise He deserves. He's made us to shine, but also to love and be loved and to serve and be served. In the environment of a football club where life can be pretty unrealistic (yeah, Mr Gucci doesn't always do home deliveries!), how did Cyril manage to stay in touch with God and maintain his desire to serve Him?

A desire to serve Him is always there. You know the truth and you have to tell others. After you know how Jesus has changed you then you just want to serve Him by telling other people about His love. You don't know what the Holy Spirit is doing in someone's heart, so you have to be prepared to share the gospel and let Him do the rest. When you're a young Christian you can get really upset if people aren't changing right away, but you have to remember it's God's timing. I didn't know Jesus until I was 33 but plenty of people had told me about Him before, so don't be disheartened, just keep going. There is a desire to serve in me because this is the harvest field; we just need to be obedient. We are the workers! As a Christian, we have a purpose and if we don't share the gospel, give our testimonies, tell our friends and families, how can we harvest? Our friends could go on not believing if we didn't share what we know with them. There is desire to witness for the Lord, to help other people, especially those hurting or in trouble.

Attempting to be the best you can be at everything seems pretty much the way to go! God is a huge part of Cyril's life; central to who he is. God is the person who has brought him to where he is now and he's eternally grateful for that. For some people though God can be a little bit of a daunting prospect. When we come to choose our jobs or hobbies, what if we enjoy white-water rafting and we need to practice on Sundays, how do we reconcile that with missing church? This has obviously raised its ugly head in Cyril's life, so how has he coped when he has had to play on a Sunday?

I think it's a personal choice, I think God understands. We're miles away from religion! God understands and I believe He says, 'I know you have to play on a Sunday, give me Saturday then.' I'm a Christian 24/7, 365 days a year, it's about giving Him your heart and soul, coming to Him with reverence and respect and if He gave you a talent you need to use on Sundays, make your Sabbath another day.

Perhaps compromise is the issue, make time and space for God in every day, in every week, and He will make time and space in yours to bless your activities. Sounds like a fair deal to me! Using our gifts and skills for God is one thing, if we are evangelists, say, but if our talents lie in solving maths problems (whose do?) how can we use them for God?

> Teach, build, go on mission, anything you are good at, God will find a way to build up His Kingdom. He calls it the 'body' and the fingernail is no less important than the brain, the pastor is no more important than the little old lady who sweeps up. Trust it to God and He will make a way for you to work for His purpose.

Read the final chapter in this book for some cracking advice from a referee on how to serve God! What can be a problem as we journey through life is not always acknowledging God's gifts, but acknowledging we have any at all. While it's important to give God the glory for the good things He does in us and through us, it's important to realise we *do* have talents. Self-esteem is different from a super ego, what would Cyril say to anyone who thinks it's easy to be humble because they believe they have *no* gifts?

> I think that is the devil putting doubt in your mind. God knows that the seed he planted could grow into something mighty and worthwhile, but the devil doesn't want to see you prosper and grow, so he throws self-doubt and low self-esteem at you. He tells you that you're not worthy, you can't do the thing you want to, you're nothing special and he tries to stop you reaching your potential. When you realise your worth is in Christ, that you are so worthwhile and valuable He died for you, then you start to believe in what He has given you. That's worth, not your job, not what you do and when you grasp this, then you how loved you are. Then you want to reach the max, want to achieve all you can, because you accept that you are worth so much to God.

Amen to that, *you* are special! Cyril had a clear goal in life, to play the best football he could and take as many opportunities he can to share his faith. He loves the Lord and he loves his football. How important has it been to develop a relationship with God which is so much more than about giving thanks for football? After all, is he so thankful now the football isn't there any more and he just has his faith?

God is gracious, I became a Christian towards the end of my career, but I was still well known and still playing. I gave my life to the Lord in the close season and I knew I needed to go public. I was playing football like a 21-year-old, it was flowing and people noticed the difference in my abilities after I came to the Lord. The Holy Spirit told me then it was time to tell the reporters I was a Christian and to explain why. After that was out I felt great, it was a huge release. I felt God used my fame to share the gospel, after all, people knew me as a playboy and party animal and perceived me to have everything; fame, money, cars, women, drugs, yet here I was saying it's not enough. I was given and still am given opportunities to turn around and say, 'I've had so much but without Jesus it's nothing!'

You really can tell from Cyril that his faith is the most important thing to him, it's wonderful. Cyril is now in demand as a speaker and ambassador for the game, not least speaking about his faith in all sorts of places, including *pubs*! Does he feel equipped to do this, has God given him even more skills?

Yes, He does equip you, but you have to get out of the boat too. There are so many levels with God, and when you get to a place of comfort He comes along and stirs you up a bit, says, 'Cyril, let's try something else now, let's go deeper'. Who would have thought I would be doing public speaking, me, a footballer and speaking out for God, but He just asks us to take a little step and trust Him to do the rest. Also, I find that one day I can read some Scripture and take something out of it, next time I get something else, something deeper. Someone said the Christian life was a big adventure and it is when you're with God, He never leaves you on your own. You can get so scared if you think about yourself, think about doing something

> with your own talents, but it's not just you, it's God's strength
> and power. Sometimes you have to ignore the criticism and the
> fears and trust God, He will bring you through.

Cyril Regis has had many highs in a long, impressive footballing
career, but it's undoubtedly his greatest personal triumph and best
use of his God-given talent to hear him share the gospel, to listen
as he tells you honestly that fame and fortune come and go without
satisfying, but a true life-changing love of the Lord lasts forever.
Cyril has won many admirers on the pitch, but off it he is using his
talents for a far higher and mightier purpose, sharing Christ's love
with our hurting world. God can use you too for this, just give Him
your heart and He will do the rest. Everyone is good at something,
that seems to be a fact, but remember when your adoring fans
(alright, your mum) remind you of how talented you are, don't
forget to thank the one who gave you the talents. Yes, you are
wonderful because He made you. Enjoy being you, *you are the best
one for the job.*

Further Scripture reading

1 Corinthians 12 v4
*There are different kinds of gifts, but the same Spirit. There are
different kinds of service, but the same Lord. There are different kinds
of working, but the same God works all of them in all men.*

2 Corinthians 10 v17–18
*But, 'Let him who boasts, boast in the Lord'. For it is not the one who
commends himself who is approved, but the one whom the Lord
commends.*

Stuart Elliott

DATE OF BIRTH: 23.07.78

POSITION: Forward

CLUB HISTORY: Glentoran, Motherwell, Hull

INTERNATIONAL HISTORY: Full caps for Northern Ireland

BEST EVER FOOTBALL MOMENT: Winning promotion with Hull, the club's first time in 19 years and scoring 14 goals in the season.

BEST EVER SPIRITUAL MOMENT: When I first met Christ, age 17, at Whitewell Church, Belfast.

FAVOURITE ALL-TIME FOOTBALL ELEVEN (*4/4/2 formation*):

	Schmeichel		
Salgado	Hansen	Ferdinand	Roberto Carlos
Beckham	Zidane	Maradona	Best
Van Basten		Rush	

FAVOURITE PIECE OF SCRIPTURE: **Jeremiah 29 v11**

Stuart Elliott
How to tell others

Stuart Elliott is a Northern Ireland international, Hull midfielder and he has a big mouth! Actually he has a normal sized mouth, but uses it a lot and it's mostly about the Lord. Why on earth does he feel the need to broadcast the fact he is a Christian, why can't he just keep it to himself?

Because of Jesus' commission in **Matthew 28 v20**. He came to this earth to save sinners, chose the twelve fishermen to carry on when He rose to heaven and today that commission passes to us. Jesus told us to go and save the world, not stay in our comfort zones. Christianity is good for us, yet when we look about we see girls our age on the streets; people already drug addicts, with alcohol problems. Jesus wants us to share His love with everyone and we need to reach out to people. **John 3 v16** talks about God loving *everyone*, and that's whom we have to tell. Everywhere Christ went He was interested in ordinary people, telling them His message. I believe if you have the heart and mind of Christ, which Paul writes about in his letters, then you will want to share His love. He went and spoke to people wherever they were on a personal level. Those twelve disciples, many of them ordinary fishermen, shared their hope and look how that spread. I believe Christ wants to use us in the same way.

Stuart has been a Christian now for 8 years and has lost none of his enthusiasm for sharing his faith with others. He was one of ten children growing up in his Belfast home and gives God the thanks for changing his life which was heading nowhere fast. God spoke to Stuart at a tent meeting in Belfast in 1995, just after his 17th birthday and this gave him hope for the first time. As Stuart says himself he'd been filled with doubt and fear.

> God brought me hope for the first time, the opposite of fear is faith and that's what I found when I trusted my life to Him and when He does that for you, you never want to let it go. His grace brought me to Him that night and it's His grace which has kept me here still.

Life on the football pitch is his job and one he is extremely good at but evangelism is his passion. Isn't he just one of these annoyingly talented people, surely we are not all to be like him?

> God is in the business of using 'nobodies'. The Bible says the wisdom of this world is foolishness with God, unless we become like children we won't get the message. There's a verse in the Bible at **1 Corinthians 1 v17**, *For Christ did not send me to baptise, but to preach the gospel – not with words of human wisdom, lest the cross of Christ be emptied of its power*. I believe it's saying that our message is simple and you don't need to be talented to share it. If you look at my life, I'm not someone who is great with words, written or spoken, yet it's the Holy Spirit in me who gives me the strength to do this. Anybody can talk about the simple message of the truth of Jesus Christ.

So telling others seems to be something God wants all of us to do, but how do we do it? After all, we don't have loads of experience. Is there a certain length of time you have to be a Christian before you can share with others? A sort of points system, with a little 'ready to tell others diploma' at the end?

> Again, God can use anyone at any time. A man named Legion in the Bible, in **Luke 8 v39**, was delivered from demons, became a follower of Jesus, then Jesus told him to go and tell

his story, share it with others. Same with the woman at the well in **John 4**, Jesus didn't look at her sins and write her off, he accepted her, then told her to go and tell her whole town, which she did and they too became followers of Jesus. She was just a newborn babe in Christ, yet she was effective. Anybody, any age or stage can tell his story!

Okay, okay, so perhaps God really does see it as important that we let others know about Jesus, after all it is a message of good news, of hope and salvation. The gospel is certainly the source of great wisdom, but what if we don't have much of it? Do we need to be great speakers, able to recite Shakespeare backwards and use words with more than two syllables in every sentence?

No way. The Lord when he was on earth just told simple stories and that's what we need to do. Moses had a stutter and yet God used him to save a nation. Do we need eloquent words? No, but if you trust in God he will give you the right ones, two words from the Holy Spirit are worth more than a thousand of ours.

God has undoubtedly placed a passion to share His message with others in Stuart's heart and he is incredibly obedient to that. Last year, while playing at Motherwell Football Club, he organised a youth event, staging rock bands and speakers at which he gave a rousing talk, encouraging hundreds to give their life to the Lord there and then. Where does he get his confidence?

Completely from Him. I was a child of just 13, one of ten, when my dad died and that shattered my confidence, I even found it difficult to speak to people. When I found the Lord and became a Christian at 17, He restored me. I ask God for help, my knees still knock before I play a match but I go down on my knees in the dressing room and I pray, that's where I get my strength. The one Christ called the Comforter, His Holy Spirit, gets alongside me, therefore my confidence is in the Lord.

God can certainly equip us for any task He has planned for us, so I suppose telling others is no different, but surely we need to prepare well in advance, you can't just start a conversation about Jesus, can you?

> We all don't need to preach, just talk. Jesus always related to people at their level, just telling them about God and His love. He expects us to do the same, using simple language. You can definitely do that with anyone, anytime.

Oops, no excuses then, we can talk about God anytime! Often we are encouraged as we speak more and more about our faith, learning to trust God to say the right thing; after all, it is really His Spirit in us who can give us the words. How fantastic is that! Jesus is alive in you, through His Spirit, and is able to put the right words in your mouth, just when you need them (is it cheating if He does it during your German exam?!). Does that mean that it's always words in your head or are there different ways to share your faith with others?

> I often give gifts. I think that tells people that you really care. Not just a present, but to do something for others, let them know you care, I believe that is a gift, and after all, God gave us the best gift He had in Jesus, so it does speak as well as words.

Stuart has a natural ability, the 'gift of the gab' if you like, and God works with his outgoing personality. However, some of us are a lot more shy than this and don't feel comfortable talking to just anyone. Is it okay just to speak to our close friends about Jesus?

> We can sometimes talk the talk, but often we can just live the life for Him. I don't always get the chance to share with my close friends daily but what I do is ask God to let me shine in the dressing room and at training. I don't need to use words all the time. If Christ has blessed us, then I don't think we should keep him in a box, just for ourselves. It's right to share with others, tell them how wonderful He is.

Life can be a rollercoaster at times and just because we are Christians, doesn't mean we get to avoid the lows as well as the highs. What should we do when there is an opportunity to share our faith, yet our life is not particularly happy at that moment?

> Sometimes, we have so many mood swings and we can be up or down. Look at Jesus though, sweating blood in the garden of Gethsemane, I bet He didn't really feel like praying that prayer, or on the cross, separated from His Father for the first time. He felt forsaken, yet He still prayed for us. Yes we can be unhappy and going through hard times, but it's exactly then, when we really don't feel like witnessing or sharing, that God really blesses us when we do. Our faith is not about feelings, it's a fact. So get by the feelings and get into the heart of God.

Life might not be sweet 24/7, but with God on our side, we have the security of unfailing, unending, unconditional love, wow! I think I want to go and shout that out loud to a room full of people, or maybe just my mum! Actually, telling our families may be unnecessary, if we are from a Christian home, they may well have introduced us to Christ, but if we are not, isn't it a mammoth task? How would Stuart advise those of us who might face hostility from those we love?

> It's very difficult standing as a Christian on your own. I know, no one else in my family was interested. We have to face hostility. It says in the Bible families will be divided, but eventually, through your persistence and faithfulness, God can turn things around. I had to face a lot of banter and they really didn't want to know anything about the Bible, but I just kept on going. When it's your family, I think you have to bring them to God in prayer every day. He can bring about change, but we have to be strong.

Coping with the close-knit bunch of misfits we call family may be one thing, but what about a rowdy dressing room? In this environment does Stuart get a real slagging from his mates?

> Oh yes, no doubt about it. I always say, any fish can swim in the flow, but it takes a good one to swim against the tide. Any one can get drunk or do drugs, have sex, but it takes courage to stand against it. It takes a strong young man or woman to

stand against it and yet we can. It's difficult sometimes and there can be lots of slaggings, but I think that I have the answers to their problems, to the world's questions and going against the tide gets you noticed and God glorified.

God often places us deliberately in situations where we can be an effective witness and it's surely a huge buzz to realise that our Heavenly Father thinks we are up to the task, wow, God knows us better than we know ourselves! At other times though, words seem to fail us, we have a mate in dire straits and the stranger on the bus is telling their life story of pain and suffering. How do we respond when people are going through difficult times? How do we tell them about our God, without being insensitive?

In the Bible, in **Isaiah 53 v3** it says, *He was a man of sorrows, and familiar with suffering*; I think this statement reminds us that Jesus knew all these things that we face. He had known His Father in heaven, yet was separated from Him, and must have spent many lonely times on earth. Jesus was 30 years old when He began His ministry, before He suffered on earth too. God had to watch as His son was betrayed, beaten and brutally murdered. If our friends are hurting we can tell them that although we can't understand how they feel, we have a God who does. He doesn't ask us to go down any road He hasn't been down, every road is God tested.

God has the incredible knack of bringing the right people into your life at exactly the right time (whew, He is awesome), some can be encouraging by their friendship, some can be there to teach you and to guide you. Is it important to have 'mentors', Godly people to compare notes with?

I believe it's important to have mentors, people to inspire us and teach us. However, it's important to get the right mentors, people who can be positive, not people who can bring us down. I think it's important to have mentors who are filled with His Spirit, people of prayer who really know the heart of God. You are the company you keep, so get around people who love the Lord Jesus.

So off we go, clued up on Scripture, armed with a prayer team and our 'how to be a Christian' books. We know our story of how we became a Christian in six languages. Do we really have to look for opportunities, or will we just wait on God, after all isn't He the one who is in control?

> I believe you should wait on the Lord. Sometimes you can rush in and put people off the Lord by ramming it down their throats. He can lead you in what to say – prayer is so important in a Christian's life and God can give you the right words and the right time to speak. He knows exactly the right moment and we should listen to Him.

As with everyone in this book, Stuart shares his faith and his company with a bunch of guys who don't always have the real picture of Christianity. Some people think God is a scary bloke who created us, made some impossible, fun stopping rules and now rubs His hands in glee as we screw up. Or that Christians are the owners of the naffest wardrobe on earth or that everyone goes to heaven if they are good or that the devil has horns and a tail and lives only in Hollywood. How do we correct this image though? How can we get the message across that it is not all about rules, it's about love?

> Again you need to shine before people. We do need to be relevant though, there's no point in telling a starving person God loves them, if we are not going to give them something to eat, and if we have the means to give them something, we should. You have to let your actions speak the message too. I think the church has let the Lord down at times; we need to let people know that He is about love for everyone, young and old. If Jesus were here now He'd be sharing with everyone, those with spiky hair, ripped jeans, hungry, young, whatever your circumstances, the message is the same. Churches need to be more relevant.

So, here we are getting active in sharing our beliefs and our knowledge with others and what do you know, we are actually starting to like it! For some, apart from sharing our stories, giving our testimonies, there can be a calling to evangelism on our lives. How do we know and is it scary?

> We are all called to tell others. Evangelism is just sharing this wonderful news we have. I can't go into a clothes shop and reach the young girl who works there, but her friend can. We're all called to tell our friends and workmates, therefore I think every Christian is called to be an evangelist. It did scare me at first, because we have to live it as well and we will be called to give an account before God about how we spoke to others about His Son, so we really ought to be praying before we speak about Him, that's an awesome responsibility.

People are the same whatever the age, we all just want to be loved, (yes, even our parents, sad, isn't it?). God has placed within all of us a need for Him, a need to return to the place of relationship with our Heavenly Father, our Daddy. We journey in this world alongside a whole big mish-mash of people, all with the same needs. However, Christian or not, there are some we click with more than others. How do we deal with our own human feelings about people, like when we find them irritating, patronising, liars, cheats or just plain pains!

> Some people really get on my goat, if I'm honest, but I'm commanded to love everyone. My pastor in Ireland used to say 'you might not like that person, but you aren't perfect and God still loves you in spite of all your faults'. I think you have to just look past the faults and look at that commandment which says 'A new commandment I give unto you, that you love one another as I have loved you'. Jesus doesn't say in your spare time I ask you, He commands you to love one another. When the Holy Spirit is living inside you, you can get past the irritations and see the bigger picture.

So we are now sharing God's truth with others, even the ones who require more effort to love, but, as ever, up pops human nature. How do you cope with a sudden desire to share the gospel in a negative way, you know, really give it to them both barrels about their lifestyle/attitude/ friends/hygiene? How can we resist using the Bible as a tool to put somebody down?

> I know I have said it a few times, but it's prayer. If you pray and are in tune with the Holy Spirit, then you don't have time to be criticising others. I didn't see Jesus going about condemning people; all He ever did was build people up. So the next time we are in church, thinking about people who annoy us, believing the Word the pastor is preaching is for them, going 'yes!' inside, then we should just hold on a minute, check ourselves and don't let His Word pass us by. The closer you are to the Lord, the more you should be like Him, an encouragement to others.

I suppose trying to see our neighbours as God does makes it easier to share honestly and truthfully this good news we have! Stuart is secure in His Father's love now and walking the walk, definitely talking the talk, yet growing up in Northern Ireland, he must have been aware of the troubles. How can Stuart use this gift of talking about God to impact his homeland, and can it make a difference?

> I think it really can. Football is worshipped in our country and God really raised my profile in my time at Glentoran where I could relate to the young people. I've been given an opportunity to tell my story, to share with those living in that place that there is a better way, that God can take a little guy from the backstreets of Belfast and give him a new life. I have a new song on my lips and I want to share it. Football has meant I can get opportunities to speak to people, I do interviews when I am home and that means my faith can speak for itself. God can use me and I want Him to get the glory He deserves.

Stuart may be passionate about sharing this good news and has been put in a position, thanks to his undoubted talents with a ball, where he can, but how does he stop his position on the pitch making him a false idol? How does he stop people worshipping him?

Staying close to God. Human nature is such that we are all filled with pride, especially the job that I'm in, scoring lots of goals, earning plenty of money, having the world at your feet, but you have to keep a short account with God. I constantly need to keep in the presence of God, keep in the prayer house, asking Him to make me humble, after all, I am nothing without Him. My old church used to say: 'seven prayerless days makes a Christian weak', and that's the truth, you must stay close to God in prayer.

If we all think back to our faith journeys, somebody somewhere had the gift and the guts to talk to us about the Lord. Whether we have been in a relationship with God since nappies or if we had an exciting, gob smacking conversion, we still had to hear the truth from someone else. Stuart Elliott is passionate about bringing God's good news to as many people as possible and he does that in an environment more used to blondes, booze and bank accounts. So how does he recommend we share our faith with those who appear to have happy lives, who seem to have everything? ·

You only have to look at the amount of suicides and alcoholic movie stars or businessmen, to see money doesn't buy true happiness. You may have a nice home, big car, lots of friends, clever mind, but inside you are always striving for something more. The only thing that can really satisfy this hunger is Christ. You might have every material possession, God has blessed me with that, I have played in front of crowds of 50 000, have a nice house, but see at the end of it all, I have nothing without Christ, He is all I want in life. Look at Zaccheus in the Bible, in **Luke 19**, he had everything there was to offer in life, but he climbed up that tree – why? He recognised that Jesus, this peasant carpenter who was coming along the road had much more to offer. It doesn't matter whether you are rich or poor, only Jesus Christ can satisfy your needs.

Wow, this guy undoubtedly has a hunger for God and a desire to share his faith. God will surely reward this impressive striker of hearts. We're not all put in places of profile or plenty, but we are all gifted opportunities to tell of our faith. God gives us everything we need to be effective for Him, all He asks is we trust Him and use His words. Come on, let's follow Stuart Elliott's lead, let's begin to talk and never shut up, lets tell as many as we can about our love of the Lord and to begin? Just open your mouth!

Further Scripture reading

Matthew 28 vs19–20

Therefore go and make disciples of all nations, baptising them in the name of the Father and of the Son and of the Holy Spirit, and teaching them to obey everything I have commanded you. And surely I am with you always, to the very end of the age.

Romans 10 vs13–14

... for, 'Everyone who calls on the name of the Lord will be saved.' How, then, can they call on one they have not believed in? And how can they believe in the one of whom they have not heard? And how can they hear without someone preaching to them?

Revelation 1 v3

Blessed is the one who reads the words of this prophecy, and blessed are those who hear it and take to heart what is written in it, because the time is near.

Isaiah 12 v4

... Give thanks to the Lord, call on His name; make known among the nations what He has done, and proclaim that His name is exalted.

Luke 24 vs45–47

Then He opened their minds so they could understand the Scriptures. He told them, 'This is what is written: The Christ will suffer and rise from the dead on the third day, and repentance and forgiveness of sins will be preached in His name to all nations, beginning at Jerusalem.'

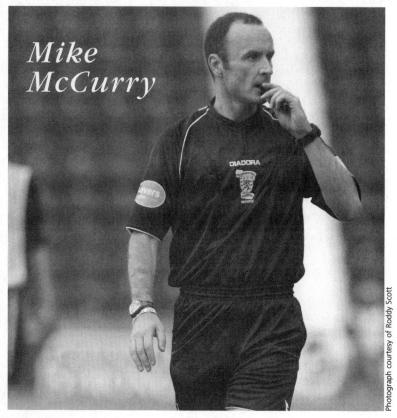

Photograph courtesy of Roddy Scott

Mike McCurry

DATE OF BIRTH: 04.06.64

POSITION: Referee

BEST EVER FOOTBALL MOMENT: Running onto the park for my first Old Firm game, closely followed by running off at the end of my first Old Firm game!

BEST EVER SPIRITUAL MOMENT: Getting saved.

FAVOURITE ALL-TIME FOOTBALL ELEVEN (*4/4/2 formation*):

		Zoff		
Carlos Alberto	Passarella		Beckenbauer	Maldini
Cruyff	Zidane		Maradona	Best
	Pele	Van Basten		

SUBS: Platini, McCurry

FAVOURITE PIECE OF SCRIPTURE: **Habbakuk 1 v5, Genesis 1 v1, John 3 v16, Jeremiah 29 v11, Psalm 62 v8**

Mike McCurry
How to find your ministry

The 90 minutes are nearly up on this book now, and we come to the last chapter, *How to find your ministry*. It seems appropriate that the final whistle will be blown, not by a footballer, but by the man in the middle, referee, Michael McCurry.

The man in black is certainly one of the most controversial figures on the field and seldom the most popular, yet the role is vital to the game. So do you need to be mad to be a ref?

> When you look at the job we do there are times when I think to myself, I must be mad to do this. When you pick up newspapers, or hear TV reports saying how badly you have done, you certainly have to be a bit different; you have to develop a thick skin so that you can take the criticism. To be able to do the job over 90 or 120 minutes in an arena where 99 per cent of the people watching your decisions are biased, then I am coming round to the conclusion that insanity helps!

Mike was born in Glasgow in 1964 (sorry Mike, had to tell) and brought up in a Christian home, his father being an independent church minister. Life in the manse was happy enough, but, as is often the case, Mike went through a period of rebellion.

> The difficulty with being brought up in a Christian home is you start to think am I missing something out there? Between the

age of 16 and 18 I was curious to see what else was out there. I wondered if I had been brainwashed a bit and I went round a whole load of other places of worship, not all of them churches. I did try things like nightclubs, other kinds of churches, other kinds of religion, but for me Christianity was always a great benchmark and after two years of looking around I realised that what I had was the best for me. While some things were exciting and different for a season, nothing had the depth and substance my Christian church life had.

Returning to his faith brought Mike to a closer relationship with God, and gave him a desire to have a relationship that was two-way. Mike wanted to know Jesus personally and he believes that is the core to tapping into God's plans for your life and how to serve Him.

A lot of people know about God and believe in Him, but there is a whole new dimension to this when you enter into a spiritual relationship. Experience is really the key. When I look back at my Christian life, there is no logic to the way things have worked out, yet because you have taken a step of faith, God has looked after you. When I was a child I used to play a game with my father where he put me on top of the kitchen table, then told me to jump and he always caught me. It's like that with God, you know He is always going to catch you, so when He asks you to serve Him, or minister, or take a step of faith, you know He will always be there. As your walk with God deepens and you take more of these steps it becomes easier. When you look back you may not know how it works, but it has, so you decide to keep going with God.

Mike has certainly kept going with God, recently giving up a successful career as an accountant to become a full time Baptist minister, eh, *what?*

For a number of years I have known I had a destiny to fulfil, a path to tread. I knew the gifts God has given me could be used in ministry, I just wasn't sure if it was full time or not. About 15 years ago many people in my church asked me if I'd considered being a minister, they said they saw the abilities and calling in my life. Ten years ago I tried to push open some doors to do this full time, but nothing happened. I thought then perhaps I wasn't meant to be a minister, or that it wasn't God's timing so I left it. Two years ago I started to think about it again believing God did have a full time position for me, I just didn't know where and when. After that I took a call from Lesley Edge, the minister at Mosspark Baptist, telling me the church had been praying for two years for an assistant minister and they wanted me to accept the position. For me it just proved that it was definitely God's will for my life and certainly His timing. There have been signs all along the path for me. God will let you know what He wants you to do, using people, Scripture, answered prayers – it just needs you to listen and for you to ask Him to guide you.

As well as having a full time job as a minister (the tabloids had a fun time with the headlines!), refereeing, being a magician (yes) and public speaking, he started the G1 foundation, which puts on Christian concerts and events for young people. So, a bit of a slacker, McCurry! People may see a personality in keeping with his faith, perhaps God was honing the thick skin required to handle an old firm match, but one way or another, Mike was blessed with a dogged determination to achieve in all areas.

I sometimes think that comes from being a bad loser. When I did play football (an injury brought an end to any serious playing plans), I had a real temper and I couldn't handle defeat. I think this drove me on to win on the sports field and if you don't like failing in anything, then you want to excel in exams too. I also believe when God starts to work in your life, He inspires you. God doesn't anoint us because we are holy and perfect, but He anoints you to become holy and more perfect. We are never going to achieve all that we should in the spiritual realm, but that doesn't stop us aiming for excellence. If God has put talents and gifts in you then you need to use them as best you can. I would hate to get to heaven and pass someone who hasn't got in because they have not made the decision to have a personal relationship with Jesus and they say, 'Mike, you never told me about Him.' Time is short and you just have to take every opportunity God gives you!

So, if Mike is a keen winner on the park and sports field, how does he transfer that to the pulpit, what makes a winning minister?

A lot of people think ministers are dull, boring non-achievers. The fact is as Christians we are called to be winners, to win people for God. Any desire I have to be successful will be transferred to the pulpit by giving God my best, giving Him my desires and letting Him define success. I said before I'm a bad loser, for me being a winning minister is one who gives God everything and lets Him lead the way and not looking for rewards on planet earth, but hopefully storing them in heaven where they actually matter.

Mike also worked his way through the various courses required to become a referee, was that an answer to prayer or part of a divine plan?

I was asked to step in one day when the ref never showed having never done it before. At the end of the game, some guy gave me the Scottish Football Association's number and told me to give it a phone, which I did and the rest fell into place. Looking back, did God have a hand in it? Well I would have to say yes, my refereeing has opened up many doors for me to talk about my faith, and sport is certainly an arena which is giving credibility to Christianity. I think a long time ago it was considered weak-willed to be a Christian, now it is given more respect. People are beginning to realise it takes courage to stand up for what you believe in.

Referees are often the fittest on the park (Mike asked me to add that) and training means a punishing schedule for anyone who also has a full time job. How do you make time for God?

It all comes down to priorities. If something is that important in your life you will make time for it. I have a full time job, the football, family life and then church life too. However, I go to the gym first thing in the morning, put on a Christian CD and often God speaks to me there. Having bust a gut and become mentally drained, I find God is very clear in speaking to me. I try and use my time wisely. Why muddle through 16 hours a day and then just ask God into the last few? Why not make Him your priority, and seek His Kingdom first. I truly believe if you put God first everything else falls into place.

Mike is another who has always been vocal about his faith; did he encounter any hostility in the world of football, specifically as a referee?

Oh yes, but most of it is harmless regarding my faith. You get some people who want to call you Bible basher, holy Joe and things like that, but a lot of people actually admire the stance you take by going public about your beliefs. The more sinister comments and threats have not been about my faith but about football decisions. I had telephone calls threatening murder, one that was explicit about stabbing me nine times with a coat hanger through my heart. I've had animal body parts thrown through the doors, windows smashed, the car damaged and lots more. I think one of God's attributes that I've come to rely on is His protection. If you place your life in the palm of His hand, then nothing can snatch you from it. My dad used to say, the only way you know how the fruit of the spirit inside you tastes is when they are squeezed – in these instances you get to know what you are made of.

So, Mike was making his way through his life, eyes fixed on Jesus, training as an accountant, refereeing at the weekends and getting involved in church life too. Before his switch to full time ministry how did God bring about opportunities to serve Him, other than constantly being Joseph in the Nativity play?

The clearest way was opening doors into schools through my refereeing. It is so difficult when you are young to get a handle on religion. What I would do is just go in to sports classes, RE lessons, and just have chat about my faith. God uses my love for Him, and my love for football and has given a credibility to the message we have.

Mike warmed to the task of speaking about his faith and using his 'job' as a ref to open doors, soon filling his engagements diary with meeting after meeting. Not all of us can talk about the thrill of a footy game to break the ice at a public meeting or do a few tricks to amuse the audience. These things aside, how do you serve God by public speaking?

Often I am asked along to talk just about football, but because God is an integral part of my life His message always comes into it. For me, I learned a few illusions to amuse the younger people I spoke to but soon adapted that into my chat and it's useful for the hecklers! As long as it is relevant and keeps the truth of the message it's great to use as many ways as possible to deliver the gospel.

Not all of us will be asked to stand in front of a hall full of people and preach or share a story (phew!), but it is important to all Christians to be able to hear what God *is* calling you to do. So how does Mike recommend we find our role for God and what if we get it wrong?

I think it stems from the closeness of your relationship with God. The more you know someone, say like your mum, you know exactly how she feels about you. I always know if I am making her happy or sad and so it is with the Lord. The more you get in tune with Him, the easier it is to determine His will. When you are willing to listen to Him, He will always guide you. If you have it in your head to be a missionary in China, and after applying 45 times for a visa, you are refused again, I think God might be trying to tell you He doesn't want you to do that.

Perhaps your skills lie behind the scenes, perhaps it's in the technical side, or setting things out before church starts on a

Sunday. Whatever the Lord calls you to do the old song says we should do it with a gladsome heart, even if it means an early rise!

Attitude comes from knowing God's purpose in your life. He wants you to have a quality of life that is second to none and where He calls you to serve Him it's for your good too. All God is looking for from us is a willingness to be obedient and the Bible says He will use us. To be the best in service you have to be the best servant. All the glory should go to God, just make sure you keep your heart soft and humble.

So there you are, God has called you to read to the elderly in the local home after taking the young kids rock climbing and life is sweet. You know you will be a pop star, preach at the weekends, raise funds for Africa and pen an international praise song, but somebody forgot to tell Satan it's a done deal. What do you do when the enemy comes calling?

I smile a lot! At the end of the day, the devil only comes when you are being effective for the Lord, or to stop you from being. Maybe it's part of the Glasgow psyche, we like a good fight! When the devil comes in you have to remember we are on the winning side, the battle has already been won. Thanks to the resurrection the devil is on borrowed time, just remind him hell was built for him and his cohorts. When it happens on the pitch and someone has a go at me because of a decision, I just think give it your best shot mate, I know the rules. The devil may well win if it was just against me but I have God on my side and He can't be defeated!

God being God, He constantly wants the very best for us and wants us to minister in as many ways as we can, ultimately bringing Him the glory and being used to bring the Good News about His Kingdom. Mike heard God speaking to him very clearly and was given a glimpse of God's plan for him, a vision it's often called.

The vision I got was in conversation with God one day, no great flashes of light or anything, we were just having a chat and I was complaining about the youth work in the church being naff and God just said if I could do it better, I should. He told me to go and do something about it. What we are doing at the G1 foundation is bringing the relevance of Christ into young people's lives. I believe He is doing a mighty thing in the lives of young people around West Central Scotland and he is just using a bunch of guys daft enough to do it, to organise meetings, discipleship courses and Christian events. There are a few ripples in the pond of God's power just now, but we haven't even seen the white water rafting we'll do, yet.

God never leaves us alone, or expects us to complete tasks we are not equipped to; His Spirit within is always there to guide and to lead. We would all really make a mess of it if we were left to our own devices (you should have seen the first draft of this book!), but when God does call you to serve Him you are always ready and always able, you just might not feel like it! So how do we take those first steps into doing God's work, how do we get out of our nice, safe, comfort zone to become effective?

The biggest thing stopping you is fear and when you realise that all you have to do is be obedient, God does the rest and the fear disappears. Often all we are required to do is to take that all-important first step of faith then God presses the action button. If it is something which would be harmful for you or another, chances are it is not God anyway.

Life in the church and serving God is just like life outwith the church – it's made up of us humans, therefore not really perfect. As Mike now ministers to his flock in Glasgow, what can he bring from his experience in life to help others, how can he help the rest of us find out this great mystery called 'God's Will'?

If people are searching for God's purpose in life for them I think I can help because I have been there. At times I felt like giving up but God brought others into my life to encourage me to keep going and to help me listen to God. I have also tried to run ahead of God or away from Him in my life and I can use these experiences to help others. As a minister there are loads of ways you can help others, just to chat through their dreams and hopes, to pray for them, to get alongside them. The Bible says when God hears prayers He answers them, so if someone needs help finding God's purpose for them, I would take it to God with them, asking for guidance in prayer. I know I am so grateful to everyone who prays for me and that has been a powerful way for me to know His will for my life.

As you begin to serve God more in the role He has made for you, apart from the curveballs the enemy might throw, fellow Christians can sometimes be a thorn in the side! It's one thing to have your vision clear in your head, Satan red carded in the corner and a sunny disposition similar to Mother Theresa, but what about those kindly souls who pray with you, but just haven't caught the same picture as you, how do we cope with other Christians (sometimes our minister!) opposing us?

> The devil is quite cute, and knows you would not take any notice of someone who is not interested in God. If you are working towards furthering God's work and bringing Him glory, discouragement from a fellow Christian is often the most hurtful. You have to deal with this opposition by turning to God and if you are close to God and following His will then handle the critics with compassion. Don't dismiss everything; sometimes God can use others to hone your humility. It's the same on the football park; you'll have a short career if you think you never make a mistake. The Bible says you have to test the spirit and if you are in tune warning bells should go off when you are under attack.

So, we have sorted out all earthly issues, what about the heavenly ones? God may have given us the big picture, but how do we know He is in every decision we make, in fact is He interested in the little details?

> In a lot of ways, it's the little things that God is really interested in. Samson was interested in the big things, like not cutting his hair, but he let all the other traits of his Godly life go and when

he did get the hair cut it was over, yet he had let it go bit by bit. God is interested in everything about you. He has plans for your exams, your partner, your friends and He delights in *every* thing in your life.

Mike has undoubtedly discovered his talents in life and for God and he has embraced the plans the Lord has for him. Such faith and commitment are an encouragement to many of us and Mike's boundless enthusiasm for doing the Lord's work is astounding (I get exhausted just reading his engagements diary for the week!) However, not all of us can hear quite so clearly what God wants us to do, so what advice would this dedicated disciple give to those of us who are getting really frustrated trying to find out if God has a plan for us at all?

God will use various ways, but it would be great if He spray-painted it on our walls. If you spend time reading His Word it often becomes clear to you. You can be at church, pondering full time ministry or a particular exam and the preacher talks about it, the light switches on or someone comes to you at some other time with a thought or insight that echoes what you were thinking earlier. God wants to give you good things, but if you feel like you aren't getting it then as long as you keep yourself available your time will come. God knows the bigger picture. A few years ago, I thought I was ready to referee an old firm game, but the powers that be thought differently. God's the same, just be ready.

Whether it's on the football park or on a mission, Mike McCurry feels he is where the Lord wants him to be. Many doors have been opened up by him and for him. God has similar plans for you, perhaps not so high profile, but just as important to Him. So how does Mike keep on going, stay focused on what the Lord wants him to do?

I always think of my grandfather who passed a Salvation Army lady giving out Bible messages every day, rain or shine. One day she was absolutely soaked so my grandfather felt sorry for her and took a leaflet, dropping it into his top pocket. It fell out one tea break, he read it, went to church that night, gave his life to the Lord and brought up his family as Christians. Now when I get to heaven, I will go looking for Moses, David, Elijah, Paul and all these people, to have a wee chat, but I will also go look for that Salvation Army lady who stayed focused and was obedient to God rain or shine.

Mike has a strong sense of God's purpose in his life and is seeking to make sure it comes to pass, so what is the secret, what is the most important thing you can do to succeed for God?

Be available, willing and obedient and then it comes down to being credible. Jesus was relevant to everyone he spoke to, kids, Pharisees, cripples, rulers. He was relevant to everyone because He believed in what He was doing and He was serving His Father, God. He made it His business to do His father's business. God blesses your work if there is substance and credibility to it.

So Mike has his mission, he loves his work and more importantly he loves the Lord's work. Is he just blessed, right place right time, or can we really be the ones to walk into our destiny, to seek the will of God in our lives. We read earlier about seeking God's will, how would Mike guide us in actually staying there once we discover it?

Once you have discovered it, you don't want to go out of it. By the time you develop a relationship with God, you have developed a discipline where you study His Word and pray and listen with Him and then it's easier to hear His voice. Some people may think of it as a circle and try to be near the edge where you can have a foot in both worlds, but when you have tasted God's love, nothing else will do. There is no better place to be than the centre of God's will.

Mike McCurry may not get every decision right on the park (most footy fans will agree with that!) yet he is prepared to put himself in the middle of it all. Sometimes, that's where God calls us to be, where the action is, with our sleeves rolled up for God, ready to blow the whistle on sin and shame and ever ready to allow the truth and light of our Lord to play the advantage. Referees get the worst treatment on the park at times, but when you have God in control of your life guys like Mike, who serve Him, have the last laugh.

Do you know God is calling you into the centre of His Will – how will you respond? For Mike McCurry, the edge of the circle isn't close enough; he's living and loving his life in the very heart of God's plans for him.

Take that step to serve Him, follow that prompting in your heart that won't go away. Talk to Christian friends and your minister. God has a plan and purpose for your life, the first step towards it is actually believing this. Secondly, push open a few doors and see how far He will take you. You can enjoy life to the max with God – He has made all things, He can even make you happy.

Trust.

Further Scripture reading

Ephesians 6 vs7–8
*Serve wholeheartedly, as if you were serving the Lord, not men,
because you know that the Lord will reward everyone for whatever
good he does, whether he is slave or free.*

Ephesians 5 vs1–2
*Be imitators of God, therefore, as dearly loved children and live a life
of love, just as Christ loved us and gave Himself up for us as a
fragrant offering and sacrifice to God.*

Matthew 23 vs11–12
*The greatest among you will be your servant. For whoever exalts
himself will be humbled, and whoever humbles himself will be exalted.*

Phillipians 2 vs4–5
*Each of you should look not only to your own interests, but also to the
interests of others. Your attitude should be the same as that of Jesus
Christ.*

Romans 12 vs6–8
*We have different gifts, according to the grace given to us. If a man's
gift is prophesying, let him use it in proportion to his faith. If it is
serving, let him serve; if it is teaching let him teach; if it is encouraging
let him encourage; if it is contributing to the needs of others let him
give generously; if it is leadership let him govern diligently; if it is
showing mercy, let him do it cheerfully.*

Game over?

There it is then, *The End*, or perhaps it's only the beginning.

God has used these guys to share their faith and stories with you, to tell of His wonderful love and forgiveness which is available for all who believe.

Football is a fantastic sport, full of passion, energy, skill, dedication, timing, training, courage and trust. Is this also how you would describe your faith-life?

Forget the bad press the Bible has received or the lies about how boring Christianity can be, it's real, it's relevant, it's life changing and it's available for *you*! God planned for you to read this book (I'm particularly grateful too!) Use it as an encouragement, whatever stage you are at. Keep on going with God, He will give you all the good gifts He has in store for you and more!

Our time on earth is so short. When I consider eternity, wow, it blows my mind away to even think how awesome heaven will be. But we can catch just a glimpse of it here and now when we get to the place where God wants us to be, right slap, bang in the palm of his hand. God really does know you and everything you are capable of, He will surprise you if you let Him.

All these footballers are succesful in their chosen careers, but to a man, the greatest acheivement they have in their life is their love of the Lord. That's what God made them for and that is why He made you too.

If your faith journey is like a football match, where do you want to be? Forever on the sidelines warming up? Joining the team but becoming a permanent substitute and never kicking a ball? Ignoring the rules and playing for the other side? Or do you want to roll up your sleeves and play with everything you've got for a manager who loves you so much He substituted His Son for your mistakes, in order that one day you could lift the World Cup of World Cups?

The choice is yours!

A prayer for you

If you want to ask Jesus into your life and become a Christian, if you want to get to know him like the twelve guys featured in this book, then the first step is to pray a prayer like the one below!

> *Dear Lord Jesus,*
>
> *Thank you, that you are the Son of God who lived on earth and died for me.*
>
> *I want to ask you into my life and invite your Holy Spirit to live in me.*
>
> *Right now, Lord, I ask forgiveness for all the wrong and hurtful things I've done this far in my life (take time to name what you want forgiveness for).*
>
> *I also want to forgive people for the times they hurt me or did wrong things to me (take time to name people you want to forgive).*
>
> *Thank you, that from now on my eternal life is guaranteed with you in heaven.*
>
> *I pray for more of your love, peace and power in my life, in Jesus' name, Amen.*

After this share with a Christian friend what you have done or go and find a church with a good leader you can talk to. Get a copy of the Bible – any interpretation that speaks clearly to you – and begin reading the gospels of Matthew and John.

Most importantly – *pray*. Come to God and pour out your heart, then listen to His voice as He leads you closer to Him.

Congratulations, if you have prayed this prayer. A new life awaits in the amazing, love-filled relationship with your Heavenly Father – your Daddy. Your life won't suddenly be problem free or without tears, but it will be purposeful, exciting and full of hope with the promise of an eternity of love and goodness in heaven – not bad, eh?

Blessings, Lorna Grady